A Leading Role in Change
A Supportive Role
in History

Maria's Resume Fall 2008 to Winter 2010

Maria E. Acosta

A LEADING ROLE IN CHANGE A SUPPORTIVE ROLE IN HISTORY
MARIA'S RESUME FALL 2008 TO WINTER 2010

iUniverse books may be ordered through booksellers or by contacting:

iUniverse LLC
1663 Liberty Drive
Bloomington, IN 47403
www.iuniverse.com
1-800-Authors (1-800-288-4677)

Because of the dynamic nature of the Internet, any web addresses or links contained in this book may have changed since publication and may no longer be valid. The views expressed in this work are solely those of the author and do not necessarily reflect the views of the publisher, and the publisher hereby disclaims any responsibility for them.

Any people depicted in stock imagery provided by Thinkstock are models, and such images are being used for illustrative purposes only. Certain stock imagery © Thinkstock.

ISBN: 978-1-4917-4091-0 (sc)
ISBN: 978-1-4917-4092-7 (e)

Printed in the United States of America.

iUniverse rev. date: 07/24/2014

Table of Contents

Topic Order for Introduction Page

In loving memory of my mother
Dolores C Rodriguez

Acknowledgments

Many thanks to my publisher for helping me.
Thank you to my classmates: Joe K, Kyle Lin, and Tashi.

Introduction

Movies have trailers, legal cases have opening and closing arguments, and books have summaries or introductions. Here is a small sampling of what each article addresses, resolves, provides insight, or information offered, to the reader. It is arranged in alphabetical order as an alternative to the chapter and table of contents date order format. Enjoy!

1. $25 Billion Auto Loan with Conditions

Wall Street failed to see and act on the kindness of taxpayer supported bailouts. This valuable lesson was quickly applied by the auto industry. They learned from the mistakes of Wall Street's. Thanks to the taxpayer-funded loan, our auto industry is operating successfully again.

2. AIG Bonus Issues

This company's desire to engage in restless and risky investment (second to Lehman Brothers) was the primary reason for the bailout. Add to that, taxpayers became knowledgeable about how they rewarded themselves for their failures. Multiple possible remedies and/or resolutions are presented. Here their actions and results are analyzed in depth in both directions. First if they cooked the books in order to receive bailout monies. Then their judgment is questioned as to why they are deserving of bonuses for cleaning up their own mess.

3. Allow Five Day Mail Delivery

Automobiles put the use of horse and carriage to the test. The Internet did it to the postal service. The use of Internet as the new express communication vehicle required the post office to acknowledge their biggest competitor. They had to deal with major sales loss and restructuring.

To compensate for the loss revenue, we see the post office attempt to use a three-day weekend rest day. It comes close to creating major problems. Many rely on Saturday services at home and the post office. They are still the cheapest parcel service for consumers. This market niche helps them buy some time but downsizing staff commences.

4. Bailout Suggestions

With big bucks comes even bigger supervision. Here the need to use financial experts in order to regain public trust is at its greatest. The creation of a consumer and financial oversight board helps our politicians regain the public's trust. The need for checkpoints, action plans, and follow-up becomes critical. We see the conflict of interest by those selected from Wall Street to answer and police themselves. Our government becomes a majority shareholder of the bailout companies to maintain trust and control.

5. Citi's Self Imposed Pay Raise

Like AIG's misuse of bailout funds, Citi continued where AIG left off. They showed total lack of consideration towards those who helped them. It apparently was not enough to receive bailout monies to help them stay in business. Their alleged unethical, immoral, and unprofessional behavior only further frustrates and angers taxpayers. It is a real life sequel to the movie "*Wall Street.*"

6. DTV transition date postponement

Managing inventory is something the government rarely does in this venue or at a mass level. Here we see why timing and planning are vital in mass production and distributions. Our government had to teach the television, media, and advertisers why timing and technology have to be well coordinated. For everyone to truly benefit, it must work like a well-rehearsed symphony. This is a part of the return on investment (ROI) that cannot be overlooked in any industry.

7. Earmarks Audits Bill H.R. 113

During FDR's years, earmarks were used to create pockets of employment. They helped create, rebuild, and improve many government infrastructures. Today, we used and depend on these without wondering of their historical importance. Unfortunately, over the years they were being used as political favors or poker chips. The misuse and abuse led to legislative change that had to emerge immediately.

8. Fire Side Chats with Constituents

As it was used by FDR during The Great Depression, now it would be just as useful for the administration of The Great Recession. There is something very calming about a fireplace and the ambiance it creates. In addition to weekly presidential addresses, there was a need to rebuild trust and improve the lines and forms of communication. Here you see the important role experts and leaders play in disseminating and collecting information. We see how communication makes or breaks leaders and followers.

9. Foreign Ministers Global Crisis Emergency Weekend Meeting

Within a week of receiving the author's recommendations to deal with the crisis at hand, then President George W. Bush meets with world leaders. This meeting would once again test our country's leadership and strategic skills. The world puts us to the test and challenges our leadership. We accept the challenge and lead with vigilances. An agenda highlighting key points to motivate and unite the country is presented.

10. Government Funded Tourism

All countries unite for a common cause. Tourism is a genetic industry worldwide. Countries are eager to promote tourism. The effects of the H1N1 (swing flue) pandemic are felt by worldwide tourism. This important revenue source encourages countries to pull together funds and resources. The Great Recession deeply hurts this industry.

Once again the foreign countries turn to the U.S. for guidance and direction. Being a part of the solutions helps us gain prompt cooperation. We see an about face by those who were quick to point the finger at us when the Great Recession hit. Now they embrace our leadership once again. Simple steps are recommended by using a platform of quality customer service recommendations. See number 24.

11. Government Operations-Pursue Bipartisanship

As earmarks were used to pay favors, the stimulus package became an all or nothing deal. Here our leaders are reminded of the time priority bipartisanship requires. We see how greater progress can be made with a small stimulus package. There were attempts at including a grocery list of side projects in the stimulus package(s). They were included to piggyback on the stimulus package. Our leaders were adamant about addressing their personal political agendas. It was taking away from the point of the stimulus package. The administration was moving towards a self-created failure.

12. Homeownership Assistant Program

Here we see a governor's passionate desire to make resources available. A homeowners' assistance program is created to aid constituents through home modification loans. In some cases, foreclosure information and/or avoidance became as important as job creation. Everyone quickly and enthusiastically embraced homeowner protection.

It became trendy to attend workshops and seminars on foreclosures and loan modification. Just as it is knowing the winners or losers of our favorite sports team. This was an excellent opportunity to use the many unemployed and pool of talented people. They were extremely motivated to use their transferable skills in a new market niche. We missed an event that made them available to work for a national cause.

13. Improving Airport Security

Protecting our airports involves more than having good TSA workers. Here the government committee responsible for hiring, training, and protecting our airports gain valuable insight. They learn of the primary cause of a high employee turnover rate and their hidden agenda. We see the important role every citizen plays in preventing another 9-11. Public service announcements (PSAs) become a vital role in communicating with travelers.

It is a form of subconscious reminder to all, to watch each other's back. They become the norm at airports. In the pass they blended into the background noise at airports and went unnoticed.

An international true life event reminds us how the loss of a love takes center stage. As in the movies, we see the emotional torment departures have on our hearts. A "kiss and go" area is created and its use is encouraged.

14. Improving the Next Press Conference on Healthcare Support

Charts and graphs became well known when presidential candidate Ross Perot used them in his presentation. Now it was our current president's turn to embrace their functionality. Even news anchors like Katie Couric stated the need for them. A simulation of events would have offered the details for healthcare reform many wanted but did not get. It would have gathered much help and garnered constituent support it desperately needed.

15. Logistics for Health Care Reform

Like utilities and energy resources, health care becomes a central concern for our government. The Clinton Administration included it in their many challenges. Our then president elect, Obama, ceases the opportunity for reform. We get a taste of the ugly truth between profits and people's health. Many finally agree to address it.

The medical and insurance industries realize they will lose their market to the not-for-profit sector. They are also known as (aka) socialized medicine. In addition, the elephant in the room "restricted coverage" is finally acknowledged. Reform begins to cover the needy.

16. Modifications to Mortgage Loan & Interest Payments

The principals used by lenders to qualify borrowers for initial loans, applied to loan modifications. This would be the quickest way to prevent the avalanche of foreclosures that followed. There was great hesitation in its implementation. Our society, as a whole, felt those who were not paying the agreed amount were given a free ride. They too had to be educated on the down side of a free ride. Yes, there is a down side.

Its simplicity was supposed to help minimize the devaluation of home values. Homeowners would be allowed to stay in their homes. It allowed for some cash flow to the banks and even back into the economy. Those responsible for its implementation did not want to go beyond the call of duty. Adding to the workload of lenders was held with great resistance. They felt their job was only to loan and collect monies.

At this point the media answers their call to duty. They begin to offer consumer education on: purchasing, budgeting, and home loans. It would take a great many foreclosures before politicians and lenders saw how it would benefit them. This becomes a new market niche for the not-for-profit organizations. It starts to take to off. We see the beginnings of educated low income homeownership.

17. Pay for Citizen's Briefing Book Advise

Usually briefings are done by lawyers. They provide an opening and closing statement to the judge and jury. It states the client's or defendant's innocents or guiltiness. In this case, our then president elect Barack Obama strategically uses this legal technique. He used it as the key source for his campaign agenda and presidential speech. It proved to be a very resourceful and insightful approach. We marvel over the massive talent and knowledgeable our country's constitutes show. They eagerly participate and provide their recommendations to President – elect Obama.

18. Passenger Bill of Rights

After several major public relations blunders, by the airline industry, passengers and citizens unite to create changes. The airline industry is forced to respect the basic needs of its passengers.' Unfortunately, it takes mandatory changes through legal means. Add to those embarrassing situations, their managerial operations competency and judgment are questioned. The airlines are required to offer basic necessities. One would consider them obviously simple, yet it had to be made into a legal case. The issue of delays and the problems that it creates are acknowledged to some extent.

19. Reversal of Bailout through the Presidential Power

Here strict paper trail and rumors of misuse are addressed. At this point the president chooses not to use the presidential power to correct the situation. Constituents feel a lack of justice and protection. Wall Street's self-imposed bonuses while cleaning up their own mess aggravated the existing anger and distrust the country feels. This is based on the congressional ratings in the fall of 2012. The country felt they had been scammed twice. First, we saw Wall Street's intent to profit by selling and hiding the facts of the toxic mortgage loans. Then they paid themselves bonuses for the cleanup. Because of this, the auto industry had to make up the distrust Wall Street created before the government or its constituents would loan them money.

20. School Postponement Form

This form was recommended to allow students time to serve their country while also attending to their studies. It would also have beneficial use by our talented working class. During this crisis, that was not war related, we needed anyone who could help in all matters of government operations. The range included brainstorming, challenging ideas, offering recommendations, and playing "the devil's advocate" as the author did many times. Here we see the emotional dilemma of choosing to sacrifice one's GPA over advising on a medical pandemic (the modern date equivalent of the AIDs HIV virus). See number 24.

21. The Second Stimulus Package

New approaches are recommended to use cash, capital, and credit. They are based on demographic social–economic status and standards. Citizens are encouraged to engage in increased spending. Tax incentives are detailed for the poor to buy products and services within their means. Rewards of greater charitable giving from the wealthiest may have provided a good stimulus package.

Here our government is reminded to include the rich in the role only they can fulfill, giving of their wealth. It could have stimulated the economy at both ends of the demographic spectrum if it had been applied. Everyone would feel they were doing their part to move out of the Great Recession and into a speedier recovery mode.

22. Stimulus – Nancy Pelosi

Given how busy the president was with the big picture, the then speaker needed to get involved in the details. Before we can rebuild America, we have to rebuild companies' training and professional traits. A detailed grocery list of areas companies were lacking is presented.

Many were from years of neglect by those at the head of companies. Others were due to a lost in the vision and mission of the leaders at the corporate level. It was a good thing that the government was willing to at least offer funding to help companies. A special fund was allocated to help find the special selling, advertising and, marketing skills a select few experts offered during the Great Recession.

23. Suspend Unemployment Tax

Unlike the wealthiest one percent, the unemployed were not given tax protection when they needed it most. It could have been because they lacked the political power players. I am referring to those who contributed to the special benefits exclusively given to the wealthiest one percent. The unemployed are put in a position to choose between paying taxes and taking care of their basic necessities.

We see a new class of welfare recipients, the middle class. They received the biggest loss of all the demographics, their jobs and investments. The most important one, which our government took for granted, their critical role in our economy as consumer, buyers, and donors to the poor. Many experienced homeless and welfare for the first time in their lives.

24. Swine Flu

Not since Aids or HIV did we see a pandemic of this magnitude. Once again our leaders turn to the general public for advice, resources, managerial insight, and involvement. We see the quick action by our leaders to avoid the lessons learned during the AIDs and HIV crises. This pandemic affects world travel. It also becomes a possible cause of loss revenue to countries that rely heavily on tourism.

A detailed action plan on handling it and dealing with its barriers is included in the article on tourism. See number 10 and 24.

Unfortunately, the author is in the middle of a school project that requires full and undivided attention. The author's involvement is postponed. Getting a passing grade trumps serving as an advisor. The president does not approve a school postponement form. See number 20.

25. Tentative Agenda for November 2008 World Economic Summit

This is the follow-up meeting to the emergency weekend meeting. It is used to iron out the details of the joint and individual countries. This letter gives specific details of the contributions and needs at the start of the Great Recession. Our government and the media are reminded of their vital participation. Here we have the opportunity to rebuild our technology and workforce. We have the occasion to replicate the makeover that former President Regan did in his tenure. An agenda with great details for both individual countries and global recovery is drafted. Numerous benchmarks and checkpoints are used to gain support and momentum in its implementation.

26. Truth, Justice and the Restitution Way

Restitution is paid for those who have suffered in a lawsuit. Given what some Wall Street did that contributed to our Great Recession, a request for restitution pay to taxpayers would be the least expected. It resembles a close facsimile to garnishing their wages. The term "golden parachutes" become synonymous with executive pay and corporate greed. This feels like a repeat of the accounting scandals and the reason Sarbanes Oxley (a set of accounting rules and regulations) was created. Yet it is not enforced because of the alleged political contributions to those in office or running for office. Once again we see the conflict of interest Wall Street and Washington have.

27. What Do You Think-Auto Industry Bailout Requirements?

We see the depth of engagement and involved our government wants and needs from its constituents. They value and use every bit of insight and information they receive. Having not included them in the Wall Street bailout, caused great distrust and mismanagement. Now they want to make up for it. This is proof of the value our freedom of speech had and continues to have during the financial crisis and bailout process. Any and all feedback, suggestions, or ideas are put on the table for consideration. Our freedom of speech is rewarded and embraced like a mother to her first-born.

28. World Financial Crisis - The Lost Letter

This letter started it all. Here one learns how critical emergency meetings are run. You learn the most important contributions and take away everyone participating must get. Techniques and format help meetings. It provides effective and beneficial results to all participants. The U.S. is put to the test in its leadership and ability to command stage presences. We visualize their take charge attitude.

Our leaders and their direct reports handle the logistics for a swift and unprecedented world leadership crisis meeting. The meeting takes place at our country's capital within a week (five to seven days). The crisis mirrors a possible financial destruction which would take years if not decades to recovery from. Then President George W. Bush is willing to hear and try out constituent advice. About ninety percent of the letter sent is recited in a speech to the country and world.

This encouraged the writer to continue helping with the numerous crises that would follow.

September 1, 2008*

World Financial Crisis – The Lost Letter

The following is a paraphrased letter of the first Emergency World Leaders Meeting. It was written between the beginning of September and the first week of October 2008. I realized I did not save it because I was planning to use it for a reality show that would help me get a job. As of August 2010, I wrote to the website www.congress.org hoping that it would be archived, but have not received confirmation of its location. So here goes. From memory I have re-written what motivated me to take action.

I share my knowledge and did my part in changing the course of history by playing a leading role in change and a supportive role in history (the title of my book) to our leaders.

I wanted to include this information because it provided what I consider to be the necessary starting point towards our recovery. It also provided our leaders with a template that highlighted our driving force to take charge. We showed to be the catalyst in crisis management that we were and still are. At that time, the U.S. was being blamed for the Global Economic Crisis. Our leaders needed to do their part as a world leader. They had to take on managing the crisis and regaining their leadership status. I was deeply puzzled as to why those experts who knew what I provided did not do their part. It was and is their job to advise then President Bush and later President Obama. I later persuaded our government to incorporate experts for the major projects that would soon follow.

I was also concerned about the possibility of a potential financial war against our country. I wanted to do all I could to return to the economic prosperity years of the Clinton Administration. I knew we had a massive problem about to expand. It could be compared to what President Roosevelt experienced during the Great Depression. Therefore, I went to work viewing this project as God's way of showing me how valuable my work experience was and still is. I hoped deeply it would be fixed quickly and easily. Little did I know God was putting me to work as something that would contribute to a historical event. It would avoid and even bigger crisis.

I figured I had nothing to lose. It was my senior year in college and having been recently unemployed for six months, I had time on my side. Little did I know that this would be the longest unemployment period of my life. It would give me the opportunity to put to use all my years of work experience in corporate America.

I also wanted to use it as an extra credit assignment. There was a need to see how my recently acquired business knowledge would actually work in real events. I was taking my most feared course, business policy. No matter how much I tried to persuade my professor, he would not accept it for extra credit. He believed I would do fine in my presentation.

I was curious to see if I could make a difference in a historical event or change the course of history. Either one would be something to put on my resume. It would fill those gaps that employers often questioned. I would also put to practice and test my problem solving skills.

To my surprise when then President Bush gave his speech of my recommendation for an emergency meeting, he recited about 90% of what I had written.

The format for the first agenda required that each world leader provide one to five items. These were specific to the urgent concern(s) of their country. Each request could not take away or devalue the needs of another leader's country.

The ultimate goals was for each participant to express what was most important to their country. It was also meant to allow them to be heard by others at the meeting. Issues would be documented and resources available provided or researched for the next meeting. The critical results and primary purpose of the meeting required a win/win approach. The point and purpose was more so to give every participant the feeling they were a part of a supportive network. This was a crisis too big for one country to fix alone and/or to fail. "Too big to fail" became a catch phrase.

A follow up meeting would address those issues that required additional research or were not addressed. The follow up would allow for greater detail and address specific areas that were not possible at the first meeting. Issues such as global warming/cooling and the economic crisis would be worked out as a group. If possible, each country would be asked to provide their expertise using a brainstorming format.

Each country would be asked to do what they could in their country to manage or minimize the economic crisis. They would have access to the best experts the U.S. could provide. The intent was to give them a feeling that there was a supportive network. This unique group would help them handle something they could not do alone. Most of them had not been a part of the Great Depression but would feel as close to one as could possibly be imagined.

As the next meeting showed, the U.S. leadership was regained. We managed to gain the confidence and support by those who were ready to "throw us to the lions."

I felt confident that a major crisis had been averted. I did my part in changing the course of history. Little did I know that I would continue to help our government for at least an additional four – to – five years. I found myself juggling full-time school courses and continuing my search for paid work.

Being a workaholic, it gave me a sense of purpose, routine, and kept me out of trouble. Never having taken an actual vacation, the six months of unemployment made the situation worse. I had to survive on unemployment, savings, and student loans. I survived during these lean times on the school's vending machines and ninety-nine cent stores. They were my primary food purchasing places.

The most important thing I learned was how open to advise and implementation of ideas our government and leaders are. I assume this is because it was a major crisis that erupted and that overwhelms them. The signs were there. Those in charge of regulations had no one watching them. It took this event to wake everyone up. No one was watching those in charge.

I know that sharing my knowledge and insight was vital. It would be my way of serving my country without joining the military. This is something few other countries offer their citizens. It is important that we understand and use our skills and knowledge. It is our responsibility to use our voices and talents to make a difference wherever we can.

Like *Rick Warren* – founder of *Saddleback Church* in Lake Forest, California says, "in order to make a difference, you have to be different."

*Note – since this is a paraphrased version of the original, the date was either the start of September 2008 or October 2008.

October 6, 2008

Bailout Suggestions

Stop having the president give announcements about being patient. The fact that his ratings keep falling should be enough of a sign to get someone else in front of the camera. We need to calm fears and begin the trust process that has been tarnished.

It would be best to have daily or weekly one hour press conferences. Use the financial experts in the various industries, government, and those admired by the public to provide the information that will regain viewer confidence.

They need to provide progress reports. Do this first daily and then as markets calm down weekly, and finally monthly. Choose making key announcements very cautiously.

People need and want to hear from the bailout advisors and managers. They can calm fears and help the process along.

Use the following list as your key speakers' line up at this juncture:

1. The heads of all relevant government financial committees
2. The chairman of the House Oversight and Government Reform Committee
3. The treasury secretary
4. The chairman of the Federal Reserve
5. Those receiving payments for the mortgage write-offs
6. Media advisors on financial matters
7. Well known investors like Warren Buffett

It is very important that Paulson does not require any protection. He cannot also offer excessive compensation to Wall Street executives. We cannot be providing special security or compensation to him. The public views those in Wall Street as part of the cause of our recession. He needs to oversee the new assigned advisor and manager(s). This would continue until we attain a 99% level of recovery.

By then we will have regained the trust from the public and world. They will consider relinquishing the lost faith and trust in the executives of public corporations. This is a big item if you want a quick and honest recovery. So have the oversight committee/board show transparency. Put them in the public spot light as much as possible.

Have an immediate emergency press meeting and discussion take place. The primary topic would be the needs of world financial markets. Afterwards we must show the world we are taking responsibility and prompt action for the crisis. We need to do our part and help our alliances calm world markets and their constituents.

The U.S. government leaders need to showcase their leadership skills to the country and the world during a crisis. This will aid our reputation and financial status. We than can contribute to rebuild the economies here and abroad.

An hour long press conference has to be a top priority with the cooperation of the media, world leaders, and financial experts.

Please read and pass along the following article to all banks involved in the subprime loan crisis: *Finally, Relief for Homeowners: BofA Settles Predatory Lending Suit*, by Aaron Task. Posted on Yahoo. com. Oct 06, 2008.

Encourage banks/lenders to follow Bank of American's (BofA's) example. There may be a need to set up a division like theirs within the bailout. We need to copy their format in order to begin the recovery process.

Better controls and a training system for Wall Street analysts' has to be implemented immediately. These would focus on the expectations and demands of public stocks and bonds.

I believe what primarily fueled this massive problem was the unrealistic expectation and negative attitude by investors. They pressured analysts and anyone else when companies don't meet or exceed their unrealistic growth expectancies. Also the excess monies given to the banks without required lending procedures and enforcements encourages lending to anyone and everyone.

This may have been inherited from the CEO's and board members who failed in their positions. Like the theme in the movie "*Wall Street*," greed has become the norm and a necessity for survival.

Financial experts need to educate analysts and the investment community on appropriate growth and debt for the various markets. Speculating counter to prosperity and growth cannot continue to gain momentum. There was a reason why it was not allowed after the 1930's crash. We forget history repeats itself.

Executive packages (golden parachutes) must be monitored and controlled by the government. You cannot afford another massive exodus of executives. Jumping ship when markets are volatile and leaving the rest to drown will no longer be acceptable behavior. I know that this may go against Paulson and his buddies on Wall Street. Your first responsibility is to protect the investors, shareholders, public, and employees.

You need to create a performance based and stock ownership method. It would determine and release an appropriate amount of compensation for any executives. This is if they decide to leave during this crisis. Make sure you and not the media inform the public if and when it occurs again. The last time this happened, the public was forgiving/ They were willing to give you a second chance to correct your proactive skills. The next time you will be expected to foresee and act promptly. They will not be forgetful or forgiving.

Please read the article *Congress hears Lehman sought millions for execs*, by Julie Hirschfeld Davis, Associated Press Writer. October 06, 2008. The article will show you what loopholes still exists that Sarbanes Oxley cannot address but you must ASAP.

I hope this information is helpful.

October 15, 2008

Progress Report on the Weekend Meeting with Foreign Ministers

My sincere appreciation and congratulations to all. This is for all who helped our president and the foreign ministers with the meeting. It took great effort, coordination, and logistics to perform this important and timely event. Please have the president and his direct reports give public and private praise to all those who participated in this critical event. They deserve appreciation for their hard work. Over the next week please include their names and/or titles as part of the president's and his direct reports daily press updates. Do it before the financial market(s) open or during the evening news.

Also please encourage your constituents to express their appreciation to the foreign ministers. They can call, e-mail, fax, or write. They can also send a hard copy "thank you note" to all who attended the emergency meeting. You can post their names and desired contact method on the congressional directory website. Please consult with them for their preferred method. This will help them see how much we appreciate their work. It was a great confidence builder and show of moral support they exhibited. We value their international recovery efforts.

I also congratulate Mr. Henry Paulson on his public statement. He expressed a more conservative and compassionate approach then last time. Favoring a protective demeanor of taxpayer monies helped him undo the damage he previously did. His comments against misuse or abuse during the financial bailout will help him. It will gain the support from taxpayers he had lost. They will appreciate seeing our monies closely guarded and meticulously managed by him. This included his direct report(s) and those who will manage the companies and funds. It will help gain the respect, trust, and admiration. It will hopefully re-instate shareholder value and a taxpayer refund. These events will further improve our stock market recovery efforts.

Please encourage the public and markets to print and post the stock market results. Start with the one from Monday. Put it in a location where it is routinely viewed. Using this as inspiration of what a great accomplishment our emergency meeting had. It will work to bust moral, energize the public, markets, and the media. This will show everyone why we are the world leader. Replace each new market up swing and frame it in a place for all to see and admire continuously.

It would help to make a public statement of a long term goal to celebrate. The goal can be shared with constituents when we reach 95% to 99% of full employment. A separate one for the stock market achievement at the 25,000 mark will be equally valuable. Use the present and future president's daily and weekly morning press time to announce each 1,000, 5,000, and 10,000 increments. It will rally support and inspire a desire to achieve our goal for recovery.

Building Consumer & Spending Confidence

Provide expert advice that helps improve the country's moral, confidence, and cognitive coping skills toward the recovery. Please have the media, television, and radio stations coordinate daily (when the stock market is below 10,000) and then weekly (at the 10,000 to 20,000 marks) motivational and inspirational advice.

Schedule them during the hours before bed time (9pm to 11pm). Include the following areas:

1. Building cognitive skills

2. Relating to and supporting each other (see affirmation list below)
3. Becoming good educated consumers
4. Reconnecting with our faith
5. Applying our knowledge for recovery

Some will be skeptical and uncooperative with our affirmations. Let them know that they can watch on the side lines. We need to help them see what the power of positive and supportive thinking can and will do.

To avoid disrespecting others religion/faith belief, ask the media to share the different beliefs our country has. Ask viewers to keep an open mind for others chosen religion/faith.

Include in this segment creating and using a **five point affirmation** that include:

No. 1 – reconnecting with one's creator/higher power, or faith based belief. For those who do not have a God, faith belief, have theologist help them create one.

No. 2 – committing to maintaining and improving one's health. Improving constituent consumer buying power, education, and interpersonal skills.

No. 3 – providing support to our family, relatives, friends, neighbors, and communities in the economic recovery.

No. 4 – providing support to our co-workers, acquaintances, suppliers, vendors, direct reports, supervisors, and competitors (we are all in this together).

No. 5 – sharing our support for the recovery with foreign countries.

These affirmations must be done daily starting now and even after we reach our goal. Ask the country to share their affirmations with at least one person per day. Ask them to offer positive feedback along with their resources.

Next Step – Press Releases

Now that you have mentioned that the monies are in the banks, please have the CEOs, CFOs, and Chairpersons' give an outline account. Have them provide the steps to be taken at each periodic interval of the lending process. Include a recap on Fridays before or after the closing bell on Wall Street depending on the market volatility.

Remember that the investors need to see how fast and how long it is going to take to recover. The daily briefings by the president, his direct reports/key staff, and now the banks CEOs, CFOs, and Chairpersons' will help speed up the process. It will give everyone a reason to have patience and supportive of the long road towards recovery.

November 5, 2008

Tentative Agenda for November 2008
World Economic Summit

To President Bush:

I have sent a copy to President elect Obama of this letter. I tried to confirm receipt. I was unable to get contact information of a direct report with a telephone number and/or e-mail address.

I would appreciate your assistance in providing him with a copy of this information ASAP. He needs as much time as you to prepare for next week's meeting with you and the world financial leaders.

Also if you can please have his assistant and/or direct report provide a telephone and e-mail address. I would like to add it to my contact list. Your participation will be greatly appreciated. That way with your cooperation, I can provide the help he needs. I can also be assured of a quick acknowledgement of my e-mailed recommendations for economic recovery in the U.S. and abroad. I made several attempts this morning. It was not possible to get someone to accept my call and/or confirm receipt of my e-mail. I only got the run around and a fax number with no telephone number to confirm receipt.

I am working on recommendations for the second stimulus package over the next two weeks. Please ask your direct report(s), congress, and the house of representatives to put the second stimulus package on hold until we take care of the November 2008 World Economic Summit.

Below are my recommendations for the next Tentative Agenda for November 2008's World Economic Summit.

Global Economic Summit

1. Follow up on prior emergency meeting with world financial leaders. Include a review of the agreed upon topics. These are the ones from the October 2008 Foreign Ministers Global Crisis Emergency Weekend Meeting. There should be three to five items as part of the follow up and starting point for the next phase. The president needs to send a preliminary/tentative agenda of each countries/regions' top three to five concerns. These were expressed at the October meeting.

This action will ensure the world financial leaders that the U.S. will build upon their initial concerns. We need a joint game plan that is mutually agreed and developed. Everyone's success out of the slow-down/recession is vital.

2. Global trade and/or business. Through a mutual win/win agreement, each world financial leader will provide one to five country, global trade(s), and/or business areas. These are areas she or he would like to receive assistance in recovering from the slow-down/recession. In exchange for this assistance, she or he will provide support for another country's or countries' one to five country, global trade(s), and/or business areas.

Every effort will be made to ensure that everyone's needs are addressed and incorporated into the recovery efforts. A chart or graph showing how everyone is connected should be presented to the media and public to reassure their inclusion.

3. Common global challenges and expenditures. Include in the agenda, cost-cutting incentives for world governments. Create a mutual agreement for funding on cost/expenses associated with global challenges and expenditures. Such items as climate cost, global warming/cooling, transportation, infrastructures, alternative energy, and world peace will be some of the topics for consideration.

The world peace section needs to be coordinated. Use the efforts previously or presently accomplished by those responsible for this area at the United Nations. Everyone needs to pitch in a portion of the cost. Together all countries will help one-another minimize their share of the cost. It may reduce their deficits and/or expenditures as well.

4. Taxes, duty cost(s), imports, exports, and currency exchange(s). Include attendees of the following categories: country's representative of the G-7/G-8/G-20, emerging, and/or third world countries. They need to agree to concessions, compromises, and a mutually beneficial adjustment. These include the areas that involve merchandise, services, and currency exchanges as part of the global recovery. These areas are a common cost/expense that is an important part of the recovery.

The goal is to create as close to a maximum profit and possible minimal expense/loss. It affects each country's taxes, duty cost(s), imports, exports, and currency exchange(s). A starting or ending point can be the half-way mark of each country's taxes, duty cost(s), imports, exports, and currency exchange(s). This would occur at the average/medium point calculation.

As each country's economy recovers, these amounts will be readjusted for the new averages/medium point(s). The purpose of this method is so that all countries experience some level of growth and recovery without hurting one another's progress.

5. Use indexes/indicators for tracking and adjustments U.S., World, and countries' economy. The financial stability department/ division within the U.S. along with the International Monetary Fund (IMF) (as recommended by *German Chancellor Angela Merkel*) should coordinate and advise the various government agencies. These include those within the U.S./global industries. Their advisement would occur when major/minor changes occur in economic indexes/ indicators. It applies for tracking and adjustments that are to be implemented ASAP. The same request will be made of other global countries. It is to help minimize the U.S. and world recession/slow - downs now and for the future.

A quarterly meeting and maintenance program needs to be agreed by all involved in the G-7/G-8/G-20, emerging, and/or third world countries. It must be a prerequisite for this to take place. At this meeting new mutually agreed upon figures for the economic indexes/indicators will be incorporated.

These would be applied to the various countries' economic stimulus packages. The stimulus packages should include what was mentioned in number 4 above. The meeting can be changed to shorter periodic intervals as acceptable recovery benchmarks, checkpoints, and time frames are agreed or reached by all.

6. Tracking of the bailout for the U.S., international financial institutions, and taxpayers. As part of the United States' effort to help global markets, it must make it a priority to share our market information with its neighboring countries and taxpayers. This information will be included in the meetings discussed in number 5 above. By making public our stimulus package for taxpayers and our banking industry, we will re-establish the trust and professional leadership that is to be expected of us.

The media is beginning to announce rumors that banks in our country are using the funds for mergers and acquisitions. Taxpayers were led to believe these funds would help stimulate the various business sectors.

Provision for the loan may have not included a required amount, be set aside for loans. The government needs to step in. Make it a requirement of the financial institutions. It is our government's responsibility to calm concerns for misuse of funds. If this does not happen, taxpayers will voice even further distrust in the government's role.

They expect the government to correct the slow down or recession we are in. This transparency will also help brainstorm ways to help world markets do their part. They need to focus on their country's particular culture, social economic status, and global impact.

7. Reporting, restricting, and managing government abusive expenditures. A new department/division within the Government Oversight and Financial Stability Committee(s) needs to include request to the media, taxpayers, and others. It would forward taxpayer fund abuse/misuse information. This will help increase availability of tax revenues and its appropriate use.

Recently the television program *Inside Edition* aired actions by unprofessional government employees. One of the companies the government is bailing out decided to abuse taxpayers' monies. They did this by using gray area business expenses. At the end of their terms they engaged in lavish vacations. These types of government misuse/abuse need to end immediately.

The state or U.S. attorney needs to recover these monies. Their assets can be frozen and any source of income they get, garnished. This applies to that which they have now or will have in the future. The funds would be applied towards taxpayer revenues recovered.

8. Use industry experts to create value added to shareholder & investors. Use Value Driven Management (VDM) to add value to our companies and use an industry expert panel. Establish and use the panel to help our businesses and individuals during our slow-down/recession. The Dean and Author, at H. Wayne Huizenga School of Business and Entrepreneur, *Randolph A. Pohman*, would be a good choice. He can guide these high profile individuals and experts. Mr. Pohman is very knowledgeable about Value Driven Management.

Select domestic and international motivational speakers, to participate and be part of the industry experts. Some ideal business experts to consider with successful records of accomplishment are: Jack Welch, former CEO of G E, Howard Putnam, former CEO of Southwest Airlines, and Ken Lewis, CEO of Bank of American. These specially selected leaders and educators will help rebuild the loss values of shareholders, investors, and businesses' net worth.

9. Offer Job Creation Credits. Require Employers' Concessions. These credits include: re-employment training, outsourcing, severance packages, and a minimum of one month's notice under acceptable layoffs. Credits given should be disseminated in installments. Require that new hires be employed at least one and a half years. Priority in hiring would be given to the long-term unemployed. They need to be selected over those wishing to change jobs, increase their income, or enter new markets and/or industries.

In addition, separate hiring steps and segments need to be incorporated. For example, a hiring order of those unemployed the longest would go first. The lowest or last to be hired would apply to those with the highest severance packages. This is an excellent time to do the best possible assessment of our industries technology and/or market(s). It is a favorable time for training. This opportunity offers the ideal timing to create the most highly employable candidates compared to any prior revitalization periods.

10. Educating consumers and borrowers on purchases, budgeting, and savings. Help our consumers and borrowers become the driving force out of our economic slow-down/recession. The government needs to request the assistance of the media. The media needs to step in and offer educating consumer on affordable purchases, budgeting, and savings. For our products and services to gain value, the consumer needs education in maximizing their net worth. With the media's assistance this can be done very quickly.

November 9, 2008

The Second Stimulus Package

The follow are some of my suggestions for the U.S. economic recovery. Some of the recommendations were previously sent for The World Economic Summit. They have been repeated here. This was done for those who did not have access to information sent for the summit.

Your prompt attention and implementation is urgently needed. It will avoid further hardships and fallout(s).

Use the U.S. census, IRS taxable, and non-taxable income records. They will aid in forecasting the various tax brackets. Apply them for recovery and economic stimulus monitors. As we approach full employment status, we can gradually reduce the amount of deductions. At that point, we can recover the loss tax revenue during the slow-down/recession and the years leading up to full employment.

Base the adjustments from the incentives for tax revenues. Provide updates on where we stand on our goal toward full employment. Include a financial stability reports. These are to be done on a periodic base.

Use tax forms and schedules

1. 1040 Form – Schedule A (Medical/Health). Allow health deductions as individual items. Reduce medical deduction to amounts over 3% (for healthy people) and 1% for those who are less than healthy. Add over the counter and alternative medicines. Include deductible items such an annual medical or alternative medical exams and health club membership. Allow a separate deduction for each dependent on their own tax form. Continue to allow a dependent deduction on their parent's form(s).

This important incentive encourages and rewards those who take care of their health. It can make them the most productive workers we can possibly develop. Use the Olympic metals winners as examples of the benefits of good health. Show this is why we were the world leader in total metals at the Olympics.

1040 Form – Schedule A (Charitable (51% - 75%). Allow a 51% to 75% charitable deductions before taxable income for the high-income bracket(s). This is for those who earn at least $100,000. Use the high income wage earners to assist the government subsidize the recovery. They already have the monies to help the poor and low income. Give them the opportunity to get a higher tax deduction. They may be willing to make additional contributes in exchange for higher charitable deductions.

This may reduce the bailout amount as well as the devaluation of the dollar. The charitable deductions must go to organizations that contribute to specific needs such as: re-employment, shelters and low-income housing, food, utilities, work training, and medical services. These specific categories would be the criteria used to qualify for the higher percentage deductible amounts.

1040 Form – Schedule B (Interest). Allow deferred tax payments on savings' interest. Base it on individual situation(s). For example if a person is fired or laid off. Employees would need to notify, within one to three months, the Department of Labor and other agencies. This would be a qualifying requirement of the change in their employment status. This will help the government and employers manage their: unemployment insurance, hiring, and re-employment costs due to industry or economic layoffs.

Allow the unemployed to withdrawal from their savings without being penalized or taxed on the interest earned. While they are unemployed, we will buy the government time to implement: job credits, retraining, and other re – employment related costs. It will also help reduce government appropriations and thus reduce the deficit.

2. Full Employment Agency. Use the agencies, which work with the Department of Labor such as Health and Human Services, and a newly created agency on Full Employment. It will report to the Financial Stability Department/Division. The Full Employment agency's primary responsibility is to help minimize the unemployed and financial hardship we are experiencing.

Close monitoring and implementation of all that affects full employment has to be closely coordinated. It will give a running start for a full employment policy to work.

3. An Alternative Credit Rating System. This new or temporary system would take into account the successful attempts by taxpayers to improve their credit. It would be based over the events of the past three to four years. Replace the current one with this alternative for those with fair to stellar credit. Base it as a percentage to their overall credit rating. Add a separate rate that compares it to the progress they have made.

Give them credit for their efforts towards rebuilding good spending and payment patterns. As we move forward in our recover, this approach will help reinstate the former credit payment system. It will resemble that which we had during our economic growth and stability of former years. The current credit rating system punishes debtors for past mistakes and events that were out of their control. This needs to change for our economy to recover.

4. Capital Investment Credits. Apply this to high-income purchases/services (minimum of $10,000 to 100,000 per year). Allow tax write-offs for purchases of consumer goods and/or services. It would apply to industries that create jobs for products and services. These are those that high-income taxpayers/rich purchase or use.

Part of the reason why the last stimulus did not work was due to the possibility that the high-income demographics were not included.

Have your financial experts work out the number of jobs to create per industries. These figures would provide new or growth job openings. It can be used to reduce the unemployment figures on a yearly base. The figures must be sufficient to stimulate an economic recovery. These can be in measurable amounts that are small periodic sequences such as quarterly, seminally, and annually.

These new or growth job openings must employ the poor and middle income. To determine the income levels of the poor and/ or middle income, use census data, market research, and their prior year's tax brackets. The investment credits can be phased out gradually once we reach full employment of 95% to 99%. We can also re-establish an acceptable, legal, and ethical value added level to the cost of living (per income bracket/category). Look for signs that the housing and stock market have re-establish the lost fair market value that promotes reasonable growth.

This incentive will help re-establish the damaged relation. These may have been caused by leaving the rich and high-income taxpayers out of the first stimulus package. They play a vital role in the recovery. They may start moving their monies and investments to foreign countries that will reward them. So do not forget them in this stimulus package.

5. Cash Reserves. These would be for foreclosures, shelters, or home improvement(s) lending.

The credit markets cannot continue to hold on to the bailout monies. The government must make revisions to the bailout package. The monies from cash reserves, created from taxpayer savings incentives, have to be loaned out. It needs to be used to help those facing foreclosed homes.

Payments would be based and deducted on 30% to 40% of their gross income. The expected mortgage payment amount will increase as their income increases and/or other basic living cost (food, medical, transportation) decrease. The bookkeeping will be handled by the banks/lenders. The profits will go towards reducing taxpayers bailout cost and/or taxes. If the banks/lenders do not like it, remind them of their role in this mess and that they can be replaced.

It is very important that the bailout monies get into circulation in the economy ASAP. If it does not, it may create further damage to the economy. It may also contribute to the continuing decrease in consumer confidence.

If a home seller makes a profit on the sale of the home, the profit will go to the government to help recover the cost. They can be given a grace period to pay back the difference if the seller makes a loss. Either way they will pay a progressive amount of principle and interest. It would not exceed a specific interest and principle amount. The amount would be figured over the current mortgage lending rate. Experts would determine the amount.

Special accommodations will cover the general homeowner categories for adjusted payments. Some of these are: medical situations, military leave, single parents, and on a per case basis

The new mortgage loans program would require mandatory trust and savings plans for their mortgage and home maintenance needs. Too many people were given loans who do not know how to budget and manage their finances. These new mandates will help them pay their mortgages.

To avoid further reducing in the home values, also include loans for those whose shelter can use improvements to maintain or improve their value.

6. Consumer Spending & Credits. For the poor and middle income, allow a tax-deductible credit based on social-economic standards for credit cards. This would be available for those with good to stellar credit scores. Allow them to deduct the credit card interest on their Form 1040 Schedule A as was available in the

1970s and/or 1980s. Allowed this credit only after certain areas are budgeted into their stimulus rebate checks.

It must also be as a percentage of: disposable income after savings, shelter costs, utilities, medical expenditures, dependent(s) deductions or exemptions, and childcare. Require documentation through electronic payments, credit/debit cards, and/or sales receipts. Encourage the vendors/markets to provide periodic online printouts for easy bookkeeping. This will help track and audit our progress when they do their annual tax returns.

The poor and middle income cannot use the capital investment credit. This alternative incentive stimulates spending at their end. It gives them a sense of do their part in helping the country recover.

It is very important that these tax rebates are not taxed. We cannot repeat what the Bush rebates did. Instead deferrer the taxes and tax average them over the next 5 to 10 years.

For those with good credit, have the lenders offer interest discounts. These would apply to weekly payments or pre-payments of outstanding balances in full. Allow their full credit card interest payment deducted on Form 1040 Schedule A. It will help them do their part to stimulate consumer spending. Offer the option of deducting the interest from future federal and/or state taxes. Base the amount(s) on the figures your financial experts calculate for growth, recovery, and future tax revenues. This will also help stimulate a recovery of our credit market(s).

7. Extend Unemployment Benefits with no taxes or waiting period. The current recovery will take an unpredictable amount of time. Extend unemployment benefits without taxing them. You will help many in this situation survive with the minimal necessary income as they seek re-employment. To speed up our employment create a re-employment listing. Include special incentives to employ those going through long-term unemployment get priority hiring.

The criteria used would be to hire those unemployed for more than 3 to 6 months first. This criteria would apply before hiring career changers who have established cash reserves. A special list created and tracked by the Department of Labor would be shared with Employment Agencies/Agents, Unions, and the Human Resources Departments/Divisions of companies. This will speed up the employment process. Give job credits for the hiring of these groups first.

8. New Mortgage Interest and Payment Budget Programs. Industry buyouts, mergers, acquisitions, and downsizing have become a new norm. Financial lenders and borrowers need new mortgage loans and interest calculations with new standards. Few jobs last 10, 20, or 30 years. The typical 30-year mortgage loan will work for a select few. The current economic situation is best suited for readjusting new loans over. Use a 5 to 10 year periods. Include adjustable interest in the package.

The interest on adjustable mortgage loans needs to be amortized/pro-rated or adjusted quarterly. This may prevent the interest rate from being extremely high. It may also promote a reasonable amount of inflation and home value appreciation to occur. Link the readjusted payment plan periodic adjustments to the mortgage payments. Base it on the homeowner's income. This will prevent the excessive foreclosures that we currently have.

Allow mortgages, insurance, and taxes to be paid weekly and bi-monthly. Homeowners will feel less overwhelmed. It will provide them a feeling of being more in control. To them their home is the most important asset. Allow smaller and frequent payments. Trust accounts and electronic payments will minimize bookkeeping cost. It will allow banks/lenders and the financial stability committee/advisors to track the progress quickly.

9. Savings Plans for Unemployment Periods. Use the equivalent of one year's income. Base it on the highest of the average prior 5 years taxable income per taxpayer. This will help improve banks and other lending institutions credit markets. We will also create important financial cushions for consumers when they become unemployed. Consumers and employers must inform their banks and/or the government when they become unemployed for a determined period. Make it a requirement of the unemployed before they can start withdrawing from their savings. This would help supplement their unemployment insurance. It will also ward off high unemployment financing.

10. Stimulus Rebate Checks for Poor, Low, and Middle Income Taxpayers. Provide stimulus rebate checks that can be done as direct deposits. For those with bad credit, use not – for – profit organizations to education and help this segment. They need to re-establish good credit and learn how to use checking/savings accounts. Offer the stimulus checks to equal one-month's earnings. Base it on the average income from last year's taxes after disposable income.

They would also need to show a 10% savings contribution and allowed funds for: shelter, utilities, medical, dependent, and childcare expenses. These deductions would be itemized on their next tax return. It would be required before getting credit for their consumer spending credit. Offer a one – to – two months grace period before or after they do their taxes. It will help with last minute spending or savings.

11. Tax Revenues/Loss. This can be better managed by allowing a reduced tax rate/bracket per demographic and/or social-economic status. It would apply to those who choose to allow the government to keep their tax refund checks. Use it to pay down the deficit and/ or recovery cost. The reduced percentage can be applied towards a future or past year tax liability. It would be within the range of 5 to 15 years of income/tax averaged before or after we reach full employment.

December 9, 2008

$25 Billion Auto Industry Emergency Loans With Conditions

The following loan conditions would help and possibly begin one industry's move out of an unusual recession relative to former ones:

1. The Car Czar (Oversight Board). It needs a group of several industry experts. The selected experts cannot receive any gains or losses from their oversight of this bailout.

The minimum expert areas needed are: sales, customer service, advertising, marketing, procurements, human resources (union negotiations and United Auto Workers (UAW) representatives), accounting, law, Environmental Protection Agency (EPA), and government regulators.

A special section needs to be formed that offers alternative training for UAW's laid off workers. Include a government representative for each state where companies have locations. They need to be able to work with an alternative training section.

Adding media representatives will be useful. They can inform the public and government from an insider's point of view.

Include a Wall Street auto analyst of the big three American automobile manufacturers. S/he will represent the companies' stocks and bonds and will look after the shareholders' interest.

The banking and taxpayer representatives will advise on the business loans and operations. The taxpayer representative will help provide the needed trust to look after the taxpayers' bailout funds.

These panels of experts will report to the Car Czar as a group. They represent each category and/or sectors' role in the success and/or failure that the bailout can offer.

It would be wise to use the media to help. They can select the best the industry has to offer. This is due to the scope of the project at hand.

They will report: weekly, bi-monthly, monthly, and quarterly to the Car Czar, their findings, suggestions, and concerns. These will be made public after private discussion. However, before they are made public, the following will be part of the private discussions:

Coaching, reviews of action plan accomplishments and challenges, concession made by the Big three CEOs, and their immediate direct reports.

Sales revenue must be reported weekly, monthly, and quarterly. Given the amount of money they are asking for, we cannot wait for a year to pass. Additional funding request and reassessments may be required. This is based on an industry expert "Fitch," (Fitch: "Auto sales to fall 10.7 percent in 2009," by AP – December 9, 2008) a goal of no more than 5% estimated sales for 2009 should be set.

These percentages can be divided into quarterly estimates for sales and one-half to three-fourths for production. God willing, if these extreme conservative figures fall below actual sales, we can always hire all the laid off UAW workers and may be even some temporary ones.

I volunteer to participate if we get to this point. If these figures do not work out, the next quarter's figures will need to be reduced by at least half. There will be a need to begin an immediate re-training, and lay off. The criteria for whom to lay off will be based on a lottery method.

The industry is not as competitive as it once was. Downsizing at all levels needs to begin. Part of the monies planed for consumer loans, payroll, loan repayment, and operations can be re-routed to training in other industries. Laid off autoworkers can use their transferable skills.

We need to cut our losses and use the rest of the monies to encourage consumer spending. This can be done by offering new disposable income percentage based on tax rates schedules. It will show taxpayers' how their spending contribution(s) will move us out of the recession.

A separate tax rate schedule can also be created for those who prefer to pay a lower tax rate. This would be in place of the consumer-spending group. These special rates will only take place after a required one to ten percent of disposable income is set aside. These would consist of savings and basic living expenditures (rent or mortgage, food, medical, taxes, and transportation). They would be deducted from the final figure.

2. Modified Work Hours. Give the UAW and other staff the option of working part-time. They would receive a percentage over the standard calculation for the 26 weeks unemployment calculated. This would help save a considerable amount during the initial first and second quarters. A mandatory rotating work shifts would need to be implemented. It can help maintain and/or improve the factory workers skill and knowledge level.

Simultaneously it would provide the maximum fair level employment for all members. This would apply even after sales do not meet or exceed the set goals. It would apply should they still choose a full-time work schedule. There needs to be a consensus that the companies will have to declare bankruptcy. If this happens then there will be warranty program protection for the few who choose to buy cars from our automakers.

3. Credit Markets. They play a major factor in what consumers will pay in interest and principal. This area is vital in the move towards improving sales for the auto industry. A more aggressive and equally mandatory reporting and results oriented agenda needs to be included. It is important for our government's participation in this. The bailout monies for the banking/finance industry cannot go to buying toxic assets. A larger portion needs to go to revitalize the credit markets for consumers. No matter how much the government pays to make the banking/finance industries look credit worthy;

those who hold the monies will be watching who pays back some or most of their debt. This is part of their primary criteria for lending.

4. New Credit System. It needs to be created during this recession recovery. Design it for consumers with past good credit who have lost their jobs. The market niche group are those who have or are making an attempt to pay their debts (mortgage and/or credit cards). Use a percentage of debts paid over the past four to five years instead of credit standard of seven to ten cycles. We will help those who learned their lesson and can once again become good customers/consumers. This consumer friendly service would require restructuring the FICO scores. Include it in the credit market stimulus package and as part of the auto bailout loan requirement.

5. Temporary Merge. Finally, as a worst-case scenario, we can require the two or three automakers to temporary merge as one company. They can continue to maintain separate market niche specialties. Create a special buyout plan for each to buy the other out. The event would take place once they recover to minimal acceptable profit level. Incorporated it into the merger agreement. Include required cash and credit reserves. These reserves along with a bonus for performance will become the new form of compensation and merit pay for all company employees. Management needs to understand that everyone in the company deserve bonuses. Sharing this new business style will help prevent a repeat bailout.

January 4, 2009

Stimulus Package sent to Speaker Pelosi

For reasons which cannot be explained at this time, employers for about the past eight years decided to minimize their company investments. They chose not to upgrade their machinery, equipment, technology, health care incentives, and educational costs. These reduced spending and investment may have contributed to our current recession.

Add to that, the recent creation of "at will" contracts. These contracts forced employees to take jobs that could end without: acceptable reasons for termination, severances packages, advanced notice to secure temporary work, mediation, and/or arbitration. Employees would also be required to cover their own legal costs as part of their out of pocket expenses. If that is not bad enough, these contracts also require them to cover the legal costs and expenses of the hiring employers.

These would be enforced should they choose to question the ethical, moral, or good business practice of the hiring employer. Any of these conditions and/or situations may lead to their dismissal. They are signing away their financial future and most likely jeopardizing their probability for re – employment.

Companies need to be taught that in order to remain competitive, they must invest in their human and physical capital on a continuous basis. We experienced many years of growth during the Clinton Administration. Back then companies invested in technology and some also invested in upgrading their industry and their human capital education.

Help employees have as close to a secure job as possible. Give them the flexibility of modification(s), and required mediation(s) or arbitration(s) in their employment contracts. Also a "back to school" clause needs to be included in the Tax Credits and Innovation Incentives. This will help us once again become the world leader in the business world that we once were.

After much thought, I have added the following areas: It provides common areas for the business environment to become manageable and operate as efficient and effective as possible. These need to be included as part of the Employer Tax Credit and Innovation Incentives for the Economic Stimulus Package agreement funding.

Employers would be required to do and/or provide the following in order to qualify for the financial infusions:

- Provide an orientation of the company's values.
- Share their vision and mission statement(s).
- Share how their job fits into the company's big picture.
- Show how their contribution fits into to the country and/or global economy.

Over the years some employers have become lazy and careless. Some companies think that getting someone with experience and a degree might be used to avoid necessary and/or work orientation(s) and training. By reinstating this basic but important process (training and orientations) we will be on our way to improving use of our employees. They can do a great job marketing, advertising, and promoting the company's products, or services. This process offers the importance insight of a company's critical role in the economy.

Based on my experience in Human Resources (HR), they (employers, employees, and HR) need to get some help. There is a need for relief from the paper work and legal issues that the "at will" contracts were designed to prevent. We will need to have employers and employees meet half – way. HR needs the legal and industrial assistant of the government's employment lawyers. They would provide the guidance to set up reasonable boundaries. This would also include: streamlining cost and re-educating themselves on employee employment concerns as mentioned above. Some of the topics I noticed from my many years of work experience are:

1. Provide employees sample performance review packages when hired (not a few days or weeks before the review) as it is currently done. They would receive them on or after the first day/week. Include it in the training process for managers, supervisors, and direct reports. This is intended to provide the best possible productivity and expectation by both sides. It will as well possibly reduce an unwanted job loss.

2. Require all employees (include those at the executive level) to take workshops/seminars. Here is a list of topics to include. Time management, creating, developing, and maximizing teamwork, understanding, spotting, and dealing with power play(s), work politics, job/career development, Value Driven Management (VDM), customer, client, vendor, and supplier relationships, job duties, description, and cross-over training, general other duties for ad hoc or impromptu events, communication skills, motivational insight, and dealing with interpersonal issues.

3. They need to be taught how to create and use: benchmarks, time-lines, check points, and action plans. Educate them on how to set and accomplish realistic goals and job performance levels, learn life and work balance, problem solving skills, create flexible work hours, incorporate educational upgrades through continuing education credits/courses (cec), ethics requirements, and monitoring.

To deal with the communication challenges, they need to be taught how to give and receive constructive criticism, and expressing appreciation in both directions (executive to direct report and direct reports to those in supervisory positions). To improve productivity and teamwork knowing when and what to delegate is essential.

Understanding business indicators for their industry is usually the responsibility of those making and delegating decisions at the top. Those who report to them can contribute greatly when they too understand this important aspect. It is part of the planning and implementing of policies and decision that are based on the business indicators.

Work politics is something few if any employer or colleges acknowledge. It is important in building and sustaining good employees. Employees need this knowledge to help them protect their jobs. It also helps deal with issues that may cause retribution from co-workers and others when ethics vs. job security are at stake.

Employees can be allowed to test out of these required educational areas. They need to show they are able to apply them to their work. If they are not, they would have to go through the workshop/seminar. Modifications to their situation can be made so as to bridge the areas that were lacking. It will provide the appropriate learning that will create a successful outcome(s).

4. The government and businesses would need to plan how the credits and incentives would be phased out. They have to take into account not hurting job security, business productivity, and/or profits. The new administration needs to have its Labor Department and Regulator Agencies keep tabs on the progress. This would coincide with making modifications as each month progresses or stands still. Businesses would need to monitor their spending and revenues, daily, weekly, and quarterly. Using this form of checks and balances by industries, would help the government stay on the same page with businesses.

5. The stimulus package needs to include a pro – rated payment done weekly or monthly. Short-term contracts by agencies and companies wishing to try out new employees will most likely occur. This is an area that has not previously been monitored. It will need to prevail given the lack of

confidence that exists. Businesses' have established an overly conservative in investments and expense criteria during the recession.

It is critical that we begin the recovery by no later than the second day of the new administration. During this significant first week the president, the media, and key experts in business, knowledgeable about the recession and recovery need to make themselves known. They are expected to lead the country through this essential phase.

I recommended in a prior letter to congress that everyone participate in a confidence building program. These need to be televised and rebroadcast often. Use other media outlets such as radio and the Internet. It needs to take place on daily and weekly sessions. The best time spot would be before those who have jobs go to sleep (prime time hours). For those unemployed make it part of their first daily ritual (mid-day).

It is very important that religion be included in the ritual. Efforts by the government, religious organization(s), and the media will be beneficial to all. Include the majority of the various religious sectors. To determine which to include, use those which dominate the U.S. demographics. The census data would be a neutral way to select. It will greatly contribute to the recovery. The format needs to include faith based business application. Show how it relates to individual confidence building for the economic recovery efforts.

I agree with Senate Majority Leader Harry Reid's, D-Nevada, comments on the *Stimulus Package*. Before our government makes the final decision on the stimulus package; include constituents' approval and feedback.

Keep the public informed of what is included and/or excluded in the package. The will contribute to the support you desperately need. The voters and the media will provide much needed information. These include detailed analysis and insight. This will help with the spending and investments in our country and economic. It will meet everyone's agenda and approval.

January 11, 2009

Fire side chats with constituents

As part of a New Year's resolution, I suggest that our key elected, acting, and senior governmental official participate in weekly fire side chats with the constituents. This is to be televised starting Saturday January 24, 2009.

We are at a critical point in the country's economic, moral, and worldly reputation. Our ability to lead, follow, and meet our challenges and competency will be closely observed, criticized, and applauded by voters, reporters, and other countries.

This is a call to action for both our government and its voters. We need to unite not just in our state of mind, but also in our desire, will, and talent to tackle our challenges. The world is keeping vigilance on how and what we do. They want to see how we maintain our leadership role during our most challenging events thus far.

I suggest a rotating shift of thirty, one hour casual and informative weekly addresses to voters. It will create the much needed support, trust, and confidence that has been lacking to date. The key administrative individuals and groups that will offer the important and timely information are: the president, vice president, speaker of the house, the senate majority and, the minority leaders (our top 5 leaders). Additional governmental agency participants include: the regulatory agency heads for financial and investments, banking, credit, automobile markets, taxes, education, and health and human services, state governors, senators, congress representatives, and mayors.

These individuals and groups should provide weekly updates of what they have accomplished, debated, discussed, discovered, challenges confronted. Include the most important one of all, what has been accomplishment and what solution they have. This will be presented to our cities, states, and the nation as worldly events. Credit should be included and given for what has and will be done within their capacity. Include that which has occurred through the help of advisors and constituents' suggestions. This shall be part of the agenda and format presented. Everyone needs to feel that they are part of the solution and are an important body of contributors.

Every week the fire side chat should be lead by one of the top five leaders, followed by each state's governor, rotating state senator and/or congress representative, and each city's mayor. The media will want their usual Q and A session. A thoroughly choreographed topics and issues should be well coordinated. Address news worthy and priority matters only. Everyone needs to understand and adhere to a professional demeanor. This event is intended to bring everyone together to inform, educate, and provide the needed trust and unity which has been lacking. The media must understand that this is their opportunity to provide guidance, coverage, and resources that will help everyone look and feel their very best.

I look forward to the first of many starting on Saturday at 3pm or 8pm EST with a rebroadcast on the internet, radio, and other broadcasting medias.

The country's future is in your hands, I hope you will accept this project as the first order of business for our country. This is part of your most important performance review and accomplishment.

January 11, 2009

Homeownership Assistant Program

I heard on the news about your swift and important task force. The New Jersey's Homeownership Assistant Program was mentioned on January 9, 2009.

I am very pleased to see that you understand and are willing to take action. Protecting and assist my neighbors' homeownership issues are very important at this juncture.

I am forwarding a copy of this letter to the top five government leaders (the president, vice president, speaker of the house, majority and the minority leaders). Our state's senator(s) and congressional representative(s) will also receive a copy. I hope they offer support, guidance, and all available resources. We can be the role model for your co-workers, our leaders, and other state governors to follow.

I look forward to hearing the detailed explanation, information, and resources you are making available. Those struggling to maintain homeownership welcome your resources and support. Use the state address and through other media sources.

I hope you will include weekly progress updates in your address to the state, counties, and the cities of New Jersey.

We can quickly inform and assisted the greatest number of owners. Please post at the locations listed below. It would be a good approach to send your direct reports handling this project to the following areas:

1. Local churches.
2. The Department of Motor Vehicles (DMV).
3. Post on advertisement billboards and public announcements (the P.A system) on bus, train stations, and at bus stops.
4. Also announcements over the P.A. system at supermarkets.

5. Hold town hall meetings at City Hall (on week day evenings, and daytime weekends).
6. Have the Property Tax Assessor/Collector send letters, e-mails, and make calls to homeowners.
7. Informational News Programs on cable and public television of your plans and services.

Through these frequently visited/viewed locations, you will get the maximum coverage. You will make good use of informational distribution channels.

If staffing is limited, this would be a good project to include as part of re-employment for the federal, state, county, and city job creation act. Our state has many individuals willing to help their neighbors save their homes. They are willing to offer their talent. There is a strong desire to work for a cause. These services will also help reduce depreciating home values and foreclosures.

January 18, 2009

Pay for Citizen's Briefing Book Advise

The state of the economy and jobs warrant paying our pool of talented constituents. It would demonstrate to the country the president elect's desire to rewarding talented people. Offer payment to the top three to five citizen briefings with the most impact or results.

Our country has many talented, innovative, and knowledgeable citizens.

By paying them for their advice, the president will be acknowledging valuable information. Some of the experts who report to the president may have overlooked.

Using our advice will give you access to valuable information. Currently citizens feel that the prior president may have not considered. It will provide a great starting point for brain storming sessions.

Note – The Citizen's Briefing Book was a collection of letters ordinary citizens wrote to President Obama when he was campaigning. It was considered a mass collection of what was important, challenging, and insightful information. Citizens wanted the president to use their insight and information in his speech and during the first few days in office.

Our citizens were eager to contribute to a president. They wanted someone who was willing to hear and acknowledge concerns. They left others did not considered important what they had to say.

It also created the framework for what needed acknowledgment. Solutions and quick government intervention during the sensitive presidential transition was vital.

Note: This message was sent to the Obama – Biden Transition Project website (www.change.gov) in 2008 or 2009. The site has been discontinued.

January 18, 2009

Reversal of Bailout Through The Presidential Power

It would be a good idea to have the president elect sign an emergency spending holt to the bank bailout on his second day in office.

Require documentation of any cash spending as of 1/21/09. By doing this, the president elect will stop the possible unethical and immoral spending, which may be happening.

From recent news coverage on the banks, which received the bailout monies, none could provide general documentation. This pertains to how and/or where the monies were spent.

We do not need another accounting/auditing misuse of funds. Sarbanes Oxley was created to prevent a repeat of financial mismanagement. Unfortunately it may not be used or enforced in this situation.

This will help save and enforce strict assignment of cash and its use. Taxpayers want to see their monies put to the best possible use.

If need be those who have spend monies inappropriately should be removed from their positions. They should be required to pay back the monies misallocated. The repayment can come out of their present and future earnings through garnishments.

Your prompt attention to this matter will be greatly appreciated.

February 3, 2009

Allow five day mail delivery with conditions

I support allowing the U.S. Postal Service to deliver mail only five days a week. Certain conditions would apply.

The government and/or the post office will have to figure out how it will handle the possible consequences of people receiving mail late. This includes the late fees and/or penalties which government, vendors, and creditors will charge. With the current economic situation, people's credit and financial relationships must be maintained. Every effort needs to be made to maintain and improve their credit and payment schedule.

If this can be worked out, then yes. If not, than they may need to work on a reduced work day. For example 8 hours instead of 9 hours or base it on a percentage reduction of their schedule time.

Saturdays need to be one of the days they are open full-time. A large majority of people work during the week in the daytime. They use Saturdays for their postal needs. They have to plan at least a week in advance the coming week's bills and other critical mailings. This is not being considered an important aspect for mail services.

They may be willing to subcontract to their competitors like UPS, FedEx, Airborne, DHL, etc. Saturdays need to be kept as one of the five – day delivery schedule.

The media has show some companies require their employees to take pay cuts. They can duplicate what some companies and one county in New York are doing. They took a pay cut. It was based on a certain percentage. It was equally distributed from management to the lowest earning employee at the post office. There is also the option of doing a rotating smaller working group per day or week. It may help reduce their budget and operating cost until the economy recovers.

The post office personnel and management need to face reality. The Internet has taken away a large quantity of their business. Also, the person or group responsible for the stamp vending machines has chosen to eliminate or reduce this form of purchase. People value their time. Their lives are inconvenienced. Requiring them to stand in line for the purchase of a few stamps will surely contribute to additional loss revenues.

Returning to offering stamp purchases from vending machines with the option of cash, coins, debit or credit cards will help somewhat. Allow stores which offer 24/7 business hours or are in close proximity to their locations offer stamp purchases. It will also contribute to the post office mailing services and revenues.

This is an industry who like the model T is ending. They will have to depend on alternative product and service lines to survive.

I recommended a while back offering pre-printed postage envelopes for the holidays.

The post office management needs to face the reality of the times. More focus on alternative product and service lines will become a priority. Workforce reduction is eminent so the government would need to offer transitional training for those downsized.

February 3, 2009

DTV transition date postponement

Please vote to postpone the DTV transition date.

Taxpayers are currently going through economic hardship. They may not be able to buy the required equipment. They need additional time to save up for the purchase.

They are currently counting every dollar for basic needs. Television may be a basic need. Given the continuing decrease in consumer spending, a converter box is not on the list of must have.

The advertisers and television industries do not realize that people will lose their main form of news and media connection. There is an urgent need for a new transition date. This is something that will have a sever affect on their revenues, sponsorships, and sales. They failed to acknowledge the major impact uncoordinated planning can have on them.

The current transition date does not give manufactures, distribution channels, and retailers sufficient time. They need time to plan, manufacture, order, and stock adequate inventory. There was no coordination between those who monitor and record the number of televisions lacking digital connection. We will experience a major loss of an important communication channel.

This is an unusual one-time massive product manufacturing and purchase. It will primarily require spending of those who are least prepared for the purchase and transition. It has never been done before.

The cost of postponing is a lot smaller than the lost of advertising revenue or viewership. This transition also affects radio. They too need to adhere to a new transition date.

By choosing a new transition date, we will ensure a smooth technological change. It will work for all involved while addressing their particular needs.

I look forward to the broadcast of the new DTV transition date.

February 3, 2009

Earmarks Audits Bill H.R. 113

Please pass Bill H.R. 113. It will protect taxpayers from any further mismanagement. Possible prevention of corruptive actions employed by certain politicians would benefit taxpayers as well. This bill will help reduce the misuse of earmark-funded projects.

After seeing the recent total lack of respect, professionalism, and misuse of taxpayer monies, we need to micromanagement those who use and misuse any monies. There has been a recent increase in their use to benefit certain politicians' personal interest. This includes anyone who is close to them or to whom they may owe a favor.

Unfortunately we need to micromanage those who use these funds for their personal interest. It may also prevent a form of payback for favors to selected individuals and groups. It has come to this, policing our representative in government. We have to ensure they are focused on the needs of the constituents they're representing and not those to whom they owe favors.

Taxpayer monies are no longer used to fund things that are primarily for their benefits. This was the original intended use of these funds.

Earmarks were once held in high regard for their ability to produce projects during the Roosevelt administration. Now they are seen and possibly used to payback favors. Now a days they do little, if any, to promote the quality products and services for constituents. They were once known and highly admired to serve a great purpose, improving our country's common interest.

Separate earmarks in the approval and funding process from other legislative. Run them with great scrutiny. This will help them serve taxpayers and not political personal interest.

A tracking system needs to be created before the earmarks are presented. The paper trail has to show that it will benefit the greater good. Its primary purpose is to benefit the geographical area and note what constituents' demographics it will serve. They must be approved and presented separate from other items for which legislative action will be swiftly approved.

If they have merit and value, they can stand on their own. It will help them pass quicker than if they are used as attachments to pending legislative.

This misuse cannot continue. Who knows how many earmarks were approved for the sole purpose of paying favors. They have become poker chips. There was no intent to serve our constituents' needs. Now we know why constituents are losing faith in our politicians.

On another note

Has anyone stepped up and provided information on where the recent bank bailout monies have gone? How has it helped the taxpayer?

February 3, 2009

Passenger's Bill of Rights

Please include in Bill # S.213, the right for passengers to reschedule a flight. This would apply if it is held up for more than three hours. Passengers cannot incur additional charges for this situation.

Please include that meals and basic sanitary needs are provided and functioning. This should not be required. But because of the recent media coverage, it has to be stated. It's sad to have to tell the airlines to adhere to such a basic requirement.

Include public announcements and offer e-mail and phone alerts. Do these at half, one, and two hour intervals with updates of departure times. This would allow passengers to use this time to shop, rest, etc. It will reduce the possible fear that they might miss their flight.

Include a requirement that the airlines' departure staff, advise passengers with ample time. The air – traffic controllers would be required to give each flight crew the same courtesy. They would have scheduled departure (weather permitting). The scheduled time would be based on their status on a waiting list. It would list them with departure number and estimated departure time. The announcement would be for the airline crew. Once the crew is ready for passenger board, then a separate announcement would be made for the passengers. It would inform them of the airline departing and the flight order of departures.

Additional boarding time for passenger would be factored into the timeframe. Use the typical movie screen scenario for the maximum time to allot. A passenger is at the farthest point in the airport running from the boarding gate to make their flight on time. The announcement would need to be done in the various languages for those scheduled on the departing flight. Re-boarding would commence at a reasonable time. The crew needs to reassure passengers that they will arrive at their destination with the best possible accommodations given weather and other available resources. The broadcast would occur in 15, 30, 45, and 60 minute increments. This would only apply when there is bad weather or security issues.

These changes help passengers avoid sitting for more than three hours, to take off, and promote good health. Causing passengers to suffer from nerve, muscle, and/or back problems for prolonged periods is unnecessary during flight delays. Putting passengers' health at risk would not be a wise use of time. There is nothing to be gained by forcing passengers to wait a prolonged period of time on the runway(s).

Airline pilots were complaining that they would lose their turn in line. They stated it was caused if they left the runway. This fear should be resolved by assigning each flight a departure number with estimated departure time announcements.

Passengers need the right to choose returned to them. Their health is something to be taken very seriously by the government and the airlines.

February 3, 2009

Suspend Unemployment Tax

Please suspend the taxation on unemployment compensation for two years. Pass H.R. 155.

With the economy the way it is, and will be, for at least two years, discontinuing taxation on unemployment will help taxpayers address their basic living expenses.

You can always recovery the tax revenue once we are in a recovery mode. Taxpayers will have the monies to support themselves and payback what they owe. They are not trying to avoid paying taxes, just asking for a hand up. Our country was built on the working class. They were taught to believe in the American dream. It's the philosophy of asset ownership and giving to those less fortunate. Now that they need our country to be there for them; it would only be reasonable to do your part.

Unemployment compensation is the equivalent of a middle income class welfare entitlement. Just like our government did not see this recession coming, so too was our middle class blown away by it. Losing a job through no fault of their own has a tremendous crushing effect on their sprit. They thrive on the reward of getting paid in exchange for manufacturing, distributing, selling, and yes even buying products and services. They know it contributes to our economy success and their existence.

This is a time to appeal to their need for financial security. They need every cent of the monies owed to them during these trying times. It will help them as much as those who are on welfare and do not pay taxes.

Remember that most have also lost their retirement and investment funds. What few assets they have to sell will not provide anywhere near what they need to get by. They were once known for being what fueled consumer spending and economic success. Now they are just a different form of welfare recipients. The only thing that puts them above those receiving welfare entitlement checks is their desire, ability, and willingness to work. They are responsible for purchasing products and services that the rich don't. It is important for them to do their part in helping the poor.

Your assistance in voting for the measure will make a big difference. It will move us forward and towards a faster economic recovery than our current situation enables us to do.

February 3, 2009

Truth, Justice, and the Restitution Way

It is time to change the way Wall Street works. There is a need for a major make over. It would apply to those that work or do business with them and how they get paid. There is an overt openness shown by the bank bailout executives and their direct reports. They show no regard for ethics and morals when it comes to our economic challenges and how much they are paid.

For starters, taxpayers want an investigation and restitution. The investigation pertains to the monies paid in: bonuses, questionable entertainment expenses, and their lavish business lifestyle (balloon salaries).

We can start with the executives. They should be removed from their positions based on the alleged intended fraud. It was committed by concealing the toxic securities and investments. Their plan to distribute bonuses is just one of the many changes urgently needed. This has to happen to begin the economic recovery.

We trusted and were willing to give them a second chance to fix the mortgage crises they created. Knowing very well that they are primarily responsible for the housing and/or mortgage crises, we were willing to give them the benefit of doubt.

These executives came to the government and taxpayers asking for a bailout. They were very well aware we would not pay if we knew the truth. We need to garnish their income and assets. They must be treated like those from the accounting scandals of the 1990s and early 20th or 21st century. We need to use them as the example of what not to do to taxpayers and our government.

It is a disgrace to see taxpayers losing their homes, jobs, and investments. All the while these thieves have lavish parties in the name of business. If that is not bad enough, they are also paying themselves unacceptable salaries and bonuses. These unethical people do not deserve nor have they earned their pay. They act as if these were the good times and they had just ripped off the biggest bank in plain view.

Clearly allowing them to manage the monies was the biggest mistake the government made. It would have been better to let them go bankrupt. Another good option would have been to give the monies to the taxpayers unable to pay their homes. After the discovery of the fine print, their intent was to treat mortgages like loan shark deals.

Taxpayers need to get their monies back and these executives need to be removed from their positions immediately. They cannot be allowed to serve on any board for the rest of their lives. Their jobs should be the last thing you consider saving given what they have done.

In addition, the current Sarbanes Oxley needs updating. This applies to the ethical requirements and operational procedures. The alleged intended fraud and corruption have to be at the top of the list of the revisions to apply immediately. These types of events warrant reason to terminate employment immediately.

The assigned oversight board for the banking bailout needs to work with the Attorney General for the country and the state of New York. This is to be considered as important, if not more so, than the accounting scandals from prior years. These executives look like career criminals of the worst kind we could imagine. They make former white-collar crimes seem petty.

Please put a presidential order immediately to begin the investigation. Swift removal of these financial criminals is necessary to begin building consumer confidence. They are disallowed from spending any more taxpayer monies, especially for questionable expenses or gray areas.

Inplement immediately a strict micro managed and limited spending guideline. Apply it at once to our current economic situation.

There is an urgent need to bring some sense of morality and respect for those who have lost.

February 9, 2009

Government Operations – Pursue Bipartisanship

Please pursue bipartisanship and compromise on the stimulus bill. Do this along with some of the other issues you will face in the coming year.

Focus on getting the unemployed back to work. Make providing them with extended unemployment benefits your top priority. If you pass a stimulus package just based on this, you will be half way toward a rapid recovery plan.

Non–work related agendas should not be included in the stimulus package. Including them in order to get them passed will be counterproductive. It will take away from the attention the stimulus package needs. Your number one top priority item, is to put people back to work again.

It may seem as an excellent opportunity to combine that which would not be approved, if it were to stand on its own. There will be confuse or devalue of the primary purpose for the stimulus package. That is, to focus on legislative that creates jobs. We have a sector that is ready, willing, and able to get our country production again.

The longer and bigger the stimulus package is, the more likely you will be responsible for the additional economic decline. No longer will you be able to blame the Bush administration.

We need action now! It is a misuse of critical time and energy. Do not continue splitting hairs over items that do not bring in the immediate monies so desperately needed. Job creation will fund entitlements and/or appropriations.

February 24, 2009

Modifications to Mortgage Loan & Interest Payments

Lenders were unwilling to work towards a half way mark in loan modifications. A court order is recommended. For those who qualify, a reduction payment plan would be incorporated, into their monthly mortgage payments. It comes with a set of criterias to pre-qualify for special situations:

1. They lost their jobs due to the economy and are collecting unemployment or welfare.
2. They fell behind because of predatory lenders' unethical contractual agreements. The terms and conditions changed without prior notice upon signing.
3. The contract did not provide a reasonable advance notification of at least 30 to 90 days. The terms and/or interest rate(s) changed. They need this time to adhere to the new required payments.
4. They are making less than 30% to 40% of their original income when they were initially approved for the loan.
5. They had a family or personal hardship event (such as medical illness and/or family death).
6. Any other conditions that shows an inability to pay based on their initial contractual terms at the time of purchase.

In addition to meeting, at least one of the qualifications above, the bankruptcy judges must require weekly, monthly, and/or quarterly reports. A court appointed financial counselors or managers would report to the judge. They are to provide status updates of the progress and/or any setbacks encountered by the borrowers.

The borrowers would be required to attend mandatory educational workshops/seminars. These include: budgeting, debt management, lifestyle changes, and financial management. These courses would include gaining an understanding on interest and credit cards. This would be a pre-qualification for all who wish to receive these special payment arrangements.

Individuals can test out of the educational requirements. They have to show they made progress paying down their mortgage and other debts. In addition, they must show the changes they have made to maintain the new lifestyle. It would be based on their new income level and newly designed financial debt payback program.

The full amount of the principal borrowed/owed will still be included in the contract agreement. The only thing that will change is the amount of the monthly principal and/or interest.

We need to calm down those who feel that these people are getting away with unacceptable behavior. Provide reminders and detailed account of how real estate housing values work. It needs to be explained to them at a level fit for their understanding. Real estate bad debt on taxpayers' credit profiles will cause damage to their credit profiles for a long time. In addition, they will be micro-managed until they can show enough responsible progress and recovery. Their progress must show that they will be considered a smaller loss in the future.

A loss to them includes the loss of their buying power and freedom. They enjoyed it but obviously took for granted the consequences of too much debt or asset ownership. This is something that those who have maintained good credit and a responsible debt base continue to enjoy.

Few complaints will be heard when these facts are mentioned and explained to the country as a whole.

Weekly, monthly, and quarterly aggregate reports on their progress (status updates) needs to be included in the president's weekly address. The key direct reports responsible for these projects are to provide a detailed (plain English explanation) periodic report.

It would be provided to the media and at constitute briefings. At first, they can be presented on a weekly, monthly, and quarterly interim. Once fears and distrust are conquered, the periodic updates can be reassessed and adjusted. It is best to broadcasted on Saturday evenings (8pm to 10pm) eastern, central, and pacific standard time. Most people are home at this time and you will get the greatest viewership.

There are continued decreases in consumer confidence. This trend requires that the president's key direct reports (state governors, senator and congress representative) along with the financial experts put together a weekly or monthly address. It will help build consumer confidence. I made this suggestion in a prior letter to all of the afore mentioned.

We need motivational speakers, faith based guidance, and financial education to help our government and citizens. These key speakers need to participate in our country's number one priority; recovering from the recession. The longer you postpone this very important process, the longer and slower the recovery will be.

Currently the media is working over-time with daily segments on the afore mentioned.

Now is the time for those assigned the task of leading our country to create a better future and begin doing their part.

I trust that you will consider this repeated advice as valuable as your jobs and paychecks.

March 18, 2009

AIG Bonus Issues

Back in January 2009, I suggested to the president using an executive/presidential order. It would require line item approval for all actions taken by those receiving bailout monies.

Now I hope you see the reasoning behind that request.

If it is still possible to do so, please make it a top priority. If it is no longer available, the following are some possible options to bring prompt remedy/resolution to the chaos that has developed:

Based on what some of the panelist on the ABC weekly news program *"This Week with George Stephanopoulos"* said last week, we do have several actions available to deal with this challenge.

1. ***Create a new firm*** that takes over the duties currently handled by AIG employees. First choice for the transfer will be the executives and/or employees who currently work for AIG. Only make the offer to those who have shown a willingness to forgo raises, bonuses, and expensive benefits. For example a willingness to fly coach or by train.

A future date can be set when it would be acceptable and affordable to return to first class flying. The second choice would be a partial bonus option. This may require the help of the justice department for an in-depth investigation. The remainder can be put in a trust account and if possible, the interest earned returned to the taxpayers.

Do not worry about the loss time and/or learning curve by those that will be hired. The industry and those that do business with AIG will be accepting of the new changes. They have insight of their unethical, unprofessional, and the abundant greed that plagues them. The government and those named as trustees for the funds must provide weekly updates to the government, media and, taxpayers. This communication needs to be both via the Internet and televised.

A minimum two weeks' notice should be given publicly and privately for these degenerates to decide. Are they willing to become the new financial model for the industry? They will have to be willing to forgo their bonuses and modify their contracts. Putting the recovery ahead of their stuffed paychecks is critical at this point.

Part of the replacement process needs to include removing the luxury work style. It was mentioned by the TV program "*Inside Edition*" regarding AIG's office in Connecticut. No company receiving a bailout is to have any luxury accommodations. That goes for work or to do business with clients. The clients will be understanding and accepting of this requirement.

Wall Street must learn the consequences of greed.

2. Cooking the books? Since AIG lead the government to believe it was financially dysfunctional, its books should show no profit. If this is the case, why are bonuses calculated on profits that do not exist? If they do exist and the executives lied, then we may be able to use violations that apply to Sarbanes Oxley. This will qualify as their intent to defraud the government/taxpayer. It provides reason to have legal action for restitution and repayment of the bonuses and/or any future raises.

As with the accounting scandals of the 1990s and the new millennium, the books need to be restated. They need to reflex the true value given the large losses, possible changes in revenue and/or alleged fraudulent expenditure(s). In addition, those who were fired or left the firm need to be held accountable financially and legally.

You have the means to track them and their assets down. Go for it, everyone is behind you.

If this proves to be the case, the IRS along with the other government agencies have legal power to seize their bank accounts. It may also allow seizing the personal assets of those current and/or former employees expected to receive bonuses.

3. Keep the current AIG format – but fire anyone unwilling to forgo a bonus. We can re-write their employment contracts. The new contracts would only provide a base salary along with restrictions. This would include having only authorized expenditures for required daily business. For example base travel expenditures on a selected set of vendors. They would offer the lowest cost available for the area within a set radius.

New contract provisions – include an access assets clause request for all employees who choose to stay or are hired. This would apply for the next bailout payment for AIG and any other company. Intense and lengthy auditing will be necessary. This will determine the degree of damage done by the former AIG management. The government and taxpayers cannot afford any more excessive payments. They have to be paid first and see to it that the mess created is cleaned up. The new contracts need to prevent any inappropriate payments.

Perform garnishments and better management of the new hire salaries and/or bonuses. These greedy people must see that they will not be given a good life payment(s). They will continue to look for ways to hurt anyone and everyone they can. It will take losing their access to questionable monies to finally see the consequences of their actions.

4. Have AIG file for bankruptcy – under re-organization. Everything will run the same except new staff will be put in place. A line item veto power will be given to an independent task force (like the one for the automobile industry) to approve every transaction. This may seem expensive and time consuming. They have an inability to use money professionally and ethically. There is a lack of understanding in the degree of damage done. They have damaged themselves and the industry. We have no choice but to do it this way.

5. A class action lawsuit by taxpayers, investors and/or shareholders – use this if the government cannot sue on behalf of the taxpayers, investors, and/or shareholders. This may be an option to executive immediately. There are plenty of lawyers who are more than willing to help.

The new choices mentioned above, will provide a tighter, more ethical, and financially feasible bonus and/or payment plan. It needs to be incorporated in due time for all employees. This will become the model by which other Wall Street firms will have to follow. It would apply whether due to a bailout or a consensus given the state of the economy and Wall Street's new "black eye."

Let them know that they will get their bonuses at a future date. That will be when it is acceptable and available. They have to wait until we have improved economic conditions. In addition, taxpayer sentiment assumes they are smart enough to forgo it now. Let us hope they too see why they have to forgo it now.

Here are some of the changes to include in their contracts:

1. Pay bonus payments only after taxpayers, shareholders, and/or creditors are paid a guaranteed minimal amount. This figure will be determined once the revised accounting rules/exceptions are factored into the gross/net profit and/or losses.

2. Include a revised contractual agreement for payment to other banks. It would be ethically and financially feasible. This would be done while still allowing for partial payments to taxpayers for funds borrowed.

3. The government has the right and responsibility to perform line item vetoes on revenues, income, expenditures, payments, and any other managerial aspect. This includes but is not limited to financial, ethical, and/or moral necessity.

Use your attorney to show due cause for the postponement of payment. In case they do go forward with their threats regarding a lawsuit over wages. Use the possible intended fraudulent transactions by AIG being mentioned by many to support your actions. For example the luxury spending that lend to the collapse and the excessive corporate pay given the amount of losses by the executives. Don't forget the lack of common sense by all involved. Acknowledge the general sentiment given how taxpayers' monies were used. This occurred while taxpayers had to cut down on their basic living standards.

A major point that everyone domestically and internationally agrees upon is their greed and unwillingness to minimize losses. This alone would advance the government's recovery efforts given the current economic crises. It would only be reason enough for them to join the rest of us on the unemployment lines. This is in addition to taxing them and/or having them fired.

People who knowingly misused investor funds cannot hold the government, investors, and/or the taxpayer hostage. They lied about excessive pay and losses while requesting a hand out from taxpayers. There are many who are unemployed and destined to work many years just to survive on their bare necessities.

If their bonuses have to be paid up to the end of this month, do it. Cut the contractual agreements immediately (assuming no other recourse is available). Make sure that they will be scared much longer from the public's perception of their greed and un-cooperative behavior than from their so-called industry expertise. They claim it is necessary to clean up their own mess.

If necessary have the media help you find qualified replacements. This can be done through a job-a-thon at the unemployment offices. We can also have job scouts throughout the country. Use televisions and website job conferences, do it immediately! It is best to have an unqualified and eager to learn new employees replace them. Their common sense and a desire to help during our current crises is critical. Wall Street's greed has created unqualified people. Unfortunately taxpayers have inherited them.

I look forward to your prompt action and employee replacement announcements.

April 4, 2009

What Do You Think? Auto Industry Bailout Requirements

"Is President Obama Right To Demand More From The Auto Industry To Receive More Government Aid?" Yes.

I agree with the manner in which the president is handling the automobile bailout logistics in order to get additional government aid.

As I have stated in my prior letters, regarding this particular bailout, we need a great deal of accountability, transparency, and realistic expectations. Taxpayers are asked and expected to bailout these firms.

The firms waited for the worst level of sales, debt, and mismanagement. This had to prevail before coming to the government and/or taxpayers for financial assistance. Now we have to demand greater accountability, flexibility, and concessions. All those who have a stake in the industry and the firms being bailed out should expect nothing less. Only the greatest requirements are to be assumed. They will have to succeed where Wall Street failed. Taxpayers are depending on them to make up for what Wall Street did not do. They anticipate return of the funds quickly. There is an expectation of a greater return on their investment (ROI) and value add to these firms. All this is presumed while operating ethically and professionally.

It may seem tough, painful, and overly demanding. The situation had to escalade to a high amount. No one wanted to participate in a preventable challenge. That is why we are having this discussion and/or bailout.

The true skills and competency of management for all firms which taxpayers are being asked to bailout must be analyzed, tested, and upgraded. It is more than their ability to get a blank check from the government and/or taxpayers. It is their willingness to do the work that they chose to postpone. It should have been done back when they only had (say for example) a $100 sales loss.

The current in-depth strategic planning and implementation may seem painful and draining. It is necessary for their livelihood and essential to sustain basic operations. Focus needs to be on getting all the stakeholders to make compromises and concessions. If this is accomplished, we will be half-way toward recovery of their industry and possibly the general recession. I hope you will all be more patient, understanding, and accepting of the work that has to get done. This is required in order to get them running a successful business again.

The second part of the deal involves getting taxpayers working again. Understand that given the state of our economy, consumers will continue to postpone purchasing durable goods. They will do this until they have at least 10% to 20% down for the asset. The tax credits, trade-ins, loss wages flexible payments, insurance, and reduced interest rate financing by the auto industry are very helpful. These innovative and flexible options show how talented this industry is when it comes to motivating its customers to buy.

So hopefully we will all benefit from their re-organization and re-structuring. Taxpayers will support their industry if they have to go through bankruptcy. The financial warranty coverage available during their recovery will also help.

Taxpayers value and appreciate companies who work hard to give back financial compensation. It benefits strategically maneuvered and well thought out business ethics, morals, and standards. They will support and encourage these firms recovery financially and morally. However, for this to happen, taxpayers must see their monies used effectively and efficiently. Wasteful expenses, assets, and debt will no longer be considered business as usual. Back – to – basics or bare necessities will become the new norm and standard for operations. It is the protocol for bailout operations.

A leaner and wiser company will be the new expected model. It will be the new way to measure, finance, strategize, and manage if any future government bailouts are to take place.

May 11, 2009

School or Work Postponement Form during Times of Crises

I would appreciate having my state representatives, the secretary of education, and the president create a form. It would extends or postponements the time for term papers and finals. It can be posted and downloaded from www.congress.org. An acceptable authority and intermediary needs to be assigned to approve the form. It can range from the president's office to the secretary of the government agency one helps.

This information needs to be included in the student's school records. It needs to be kept confidential for a set period. Only the required government authority responsible for approving, signing, the student's professors, and school administration should be privy to this information. Everyone would be required to sign confidentiality agreements.

For the work place, the employee needs similar immunity and procedures through legal, human resources, and their immediate supervisor.

This form will offer people the necessary protection and time. It encourages them to volunteer their time to serve our country outside of the military. This allows them additional time to complete school or work related materials. These would consist of term papers, tests, quizzes, finals, etc. The primary use is for situations where one has to postpone school or work responsibilities. We need to make use of our country's talents. They need to be available to help our government when there is a crisis. Their expertise would pre-qualify their eligibility to use the form. The event would take place during the afore mentioned. It may also occur when there is a time sensitive conflicting schedules at school or work.

This will give citizens the opportunity to serve our country beyond the military. It is important that our citizen feel they can be available in a time of crises. Our government need to protect their GPA, financial aid, or course requirements. We need to be in a position where we can do both. The ability to offer priority to our country's health and well-being cannot be ignored. Our educational or work responsibilities cannot be sacrificed for the good of our country. We can work for the benefit of both.

I never thought I could serve my country. I saw the value and use my work and education has provided the country and our leaders. This has occurred since the beginning of the recession (Fall 2008).

I look forward to the president's and/or the secretary of education's announcement of this form before school starts in the fall (September 2009).

I appreciate the update on the credit card and mortgage legislative recently passed.

Credit Card Holders' Bill of Rights & Predatory Lending

The credit card industry has a major degree of monopoly. They may have shown abusive power. These changes will protect and encourage responsible credit card use. The industry can still make reasonable profits.

Within the next six month to a year, this bill needs to be reviewed. Possible additional revisions and limitations may be needed. For example, credit card companies need to do away with the fine print they have long used and created. A minimum required 10-point font in Arial or Times New Roman should be required. This is the area where they usually hide critical information that hurts credit users the most.

The other major reform needed is similar to what currently exists relating to the utility companies. The credit card industry affects all industries that buy, sell, or manufacture products and services to consumers. Their various revenues sources (besides interest income and sales) need to be monitored and/or regulated. An example would be their entry into the insurance industry. This was not allowed under Glass – Steagall.

Consumers may have stopped buying partly because of the excessive new business lines they are being bombarded by the banking industry. They have entered these new revenue sources and tried to force its customers to buy. These new lines of products and services are like what the mortgage predators put in their fine print of mortgage contracts. Their intent is to keep consumers in debt for as long as possible.

On another note, I apologize for not getting back to you (my state representatives, and the president) about the swine flu (H1N1) crisis management. I had finals, and/or term papers during this and last month. You all did a great job of handling the crisis. I will send my recommendations for follow-up and planning. This is if there is other similar crises ASAP. I am catching up on your e-mails.

June 2, 2009

Swine Flu (H1N1)

Here are my recommendations to handle the pandemic.

Have our experts help Mexico inform our citizens, our boarders, and the international countries. They need to hear their latest actions. Keep them informed of our efforts in managing and minimizing the damage this pandemic can do. Show what measures have been taken. Here are two. Specify what is being done to keep our pig food safe and clean. What preventive measures are in place to avoid contamination.

Do a joint press conference with Mexico's Health Leaders about their efforts. Include their input on what help they need.

Share what measures we are taking with them. Film their progress for the U.S. and world coverage. They need our support, guidance, and experts.

The U.S. and Mexico's leaders, employers, local merchants, hospitals, and clinics need to show their support, readiness, and managerial skills. This is a local, national, and international health challenge. Our government will need to closely watch, monitor, and implement ways to deal with the additional loss of revenue. Don't forget the necessary interaction with those quarantined.

If there is no form of home schooling (for those quarantined) you need to get those school officials the help to implement it immediately. This applies to those with and without computers. We don't want to fall too far behind in their educational curriculum. Remember that we need to use this down time effectively. Use it to get as many citizens as educated as possible. We need to make up for the loss time during our current recession.

June 18, 2009

Promote Tourism with Government Funds

I agree with the bill to promote tourism during the summer to the U.S. Please also consider a separate or joint bill. It would be with the countries to which we will be advertising tourism. Create a similar bill and budget for our U.S. residents to travel to their countries. Include travel logistics for a speedy one-stop government or business locations. Include passport processing and travel funding.

Implement in the most effective and efficient manner interpreter services for foreign tourist at the following locations:

Foreign tourist drop off and pickup points – these include airports, hotels, car rentals, tourist destination attractions, and entertainment locations.

My final recommendations relate to immunization and customs matters. Provide a bilingual reference card that state what immunizations visitors to our country will need. Use locations at travel agencies, currency exchanges, vendors, airports, and foreign country medical locations. This can be the main point of informational distribution.

We want our tourists to experience minimal inconveniences when exporting our products. We need to do whatever it takes to enhance our country's business sales. Work with customs to populate the exporting forms at vendor locations. By improving our customs department/division at airports, our foreign travelers will want to return. Provide value to our quality customer service. Offer phone or e-mail alerts to our visitors. Include them at the foreign locations mentioned above. Make them specific to the products they can and cannot export. For those requiring special packaging, work with the post office and parcel post companies to assist them in this phase.

These services offer our country's businesses the opportunity to gain new and returning tourists. It will help some of our struggling businesses during our economic recovery period.

Given the worldwide outbreak of the H1N1 (Swine Flu), we need to have the best customer service possible that promotes tourism to all countries. All countries need to do their part in promoting tourism and dealing with this new pandemic. Offer them the education for treatment and/or prevention. This will encourage them to visit our country. Show them we will comfort their fears and address their medical needs and/or concerns.

We want to leave tourists with a great impression of our customer service and hospitality.

June 24, 2009

Citi's Self Imposed Pay Raise

I disagree with the self – imposed "salary raises" Citi used to raise the income of its employees. They are using a back door approach. This is their way of making up for the executive pay raises taxpayers voted down.

Through its own admission, they "reported SIX straight quarterly (that is one year and two months) losses totaling nearly $30 billion." *Citi boosting salaries to offset lower bonuses* By Stephen Bernard, AP Business Writer, Wednesday June 24, 2009. AP Business Writer Ieva M. Augstums in Charlotte, N.C. contributed to this report.

These losses are reason enough to freeze all financial compensation to everyone at the company. This should occur until they are profitable. The person or group making such a decision shows questionable competency. They are not interested in the cost to taxpayers. There continues to be this belief that they are deserving of a raise no matter how bad it gets.

It looks like the government is going to have to micro-manage. This applies to all financial decision when it comes to rewarding bad behavior on taxpayers' backs.

The media stated this loophole was not covered in the current or future contract in the bank bailout. Our government will now have to add even restrictor contractual agreement going forward. Our leadership requires the right to amend as we go forward. This is in addition to making retroactive changes when necessary.

This new change will allow collection of the monies. The self imposed entitlement pay raise will cost taxpayers in the TARP repayment plan. The present and future cost of this additional expense would be included in the revised contract.

Just because it was budgeted as part of the staffing pay does not mean they are deserving of it. It is one thing to budget and actually earn it. But when such large losses continue to happen, the monies should go toward repaying the taxpayer's loan. It could also be held in a trust. The additional monies included in the bailout repayment would continue. It would continue until we see a decreasing loss or increasing profits. This time there would be audited financials to confirm the books were not altered.

They use the excuse that they are "loosing talent to the competition." Somehow taxpayers are expected to agree to finance this "payment for so called superior talent." It is not acceptable, ethical, or professional behavior that anyone would want to finance. There are more than one million (conservative estimate) people unemployed. It is unacceptable for management to claim that they cannot find a replacement for the same or lesser level of pay. This is clearly a sample of the degree of greed. It runs deep within the veins of those who work as direct reports to the executives we recently had to discipline.

We do not need to think twice to allow these people to touch anymore taxpayer monies. They need to be removed and replaced with any one of the several millions who are unemployed. I am sure there is someone or group out there qualified. They would be willing and happy to work for the same or even a lower salary. These managers are trying to bribe those who have led them to believe they must stay to fix the very problems they created.

One of the most important goals of management's responsibilities is to cross-train and have replacements for these situations. I doubt if this was the norm during good times. But if it was not, now we know one more reason why these managers need to be trained to have common sense.

The managers may need to be replaced along with those asking for a raise. It must happen after they clean up the mess and/or produce a good return for taxpayers. They seem to forget how many are unemployed, homeless, or close to moving towards welfare.

It was the executive compensation packages "golden parachutes," that first got our attention of the misuse of corporate funds. It rewarded unacceptable, unethical, and/or unprofessional behavior. Now we see that the direct reports have been modeled in the vision and standards of their superiors.

I was all for compensating the employees' hard work. After seeing the publicly showcased bias pay for risk and carelessness behavior; I deeply regret even thinking they deserved to have jobs. Those who were witness to the consequences, of greed and reckless behavior, would focus their efforts on cleaning up the mess. This would apply even if it were their supervisors. Unfortunately I was wrong.

These people should be grateful to have a job. I am once again enlightened to the degree of poor common sense taught by this industry and its executives. It will take the personal experience of loosing not just their pay but their reputation. Then they may get the importance of being a productive and conscientious person. Their actions will cause taxpayers long term suffering. They might get it when they join the rest of us on the unemployment lines. Some may have to move down an additional level (welfare).

This event reminds me of an antidote I read in Marshall Sylver's book *Passion, Profit, and Power*, Chapter 8 – The Seven Strategies of Passionate Relationships. A cigar smoker insures an expensive set of cigars. He purchases fire insurance coverage. After smoking them, he files a claim against the insurance company. The judge grants him the claim. Upon receiving the check for the alleged loss, the insurance company has him arrested for arson.

I hope karma does not have to catch up to them. It is obvious they lack basic intelligence and/or common sense when asking or demanding a raise. Claiming to be superior beings then the rest of the country is not something the country will accept. Once again I remind those in charge of the taxpayers' financed bailouts. Taxpayers will be more than happy to remove or replace those working on the clean up. They are willing to deal with the learning curve. Taxpayers know it is to be expected when hiring acceptable, ethical, and/or professional people.

We want bailout monies to go to clean up the mess. It has cost jobs, industry downturns, and exorbitant unemployment. There are many who would be happy to take these jobs. They are truly talented individuals. They make no bulling demands or posses an "I am better than anyone else and I will blackmail if I have to" attitude.

I am all for giving everyone cleaning up this mess, a raise, bonus, and even a paid vacation. But it can only happen in due time. That time not being the present and/or immediate future.

July 13, 2009

Logistics for Healthcare Reform

The next healthcare reform town hall update needs to include a follow up. Include what were the key segments discussed and items tentatively agreed upon earlier this year.

This needs to take place ASAP but before the next government recess. The public will listen and participate more actively on this issue if it is televised. It may have been published on the Internet for public viewing. People will take an active role when it is broken down into sections. They need time in between to discuss, ponder, and address new questions or clarify existing ones. This is not an easy subject to address at one meeting. Support will happen for the reform. That will be when they feel that most of the information has been provided. They need to have their questions and concerns acknowledged along with a mutually beneficial agenda creation.

Some of the key segments are:

1. Drug manufactures.
2. Alternative and contemporary medicine.
3. Hospitals and community clinics.
4. Diagnostic and lab work firms.
5. Private and HMO doctors, surgeons, and specialist groups.
6. Present a sample of the tentative government administration responsible for the public funded new heath care system.

Hospitals and drug manufactures have offered a reduce cost coverage to the government. Now it will be expected of those mentioned in the other segments. There will probably be some kind of conflict between the drug manufacturers and the alternative and contemporary medical industry. They compete with each other very aggressively. Information about non-traditional insurance for the alternative and contemporary medicine is currently limited. This will be a vital area for concessions and compromises.

A sample draft presentation for the public's understanding needs to be included. You need voter support. Include a walkthrough of how, who, when, what, where, and why for its implementation, funding, and compliance.

For example, how will the sample initial cluster of uninsured or transfers from the private sector be screened, documented, examined, and charged? Who will get to go first? Do we do a lottery by: age, illness, or home address? Will some other criteria have precedence? What will be done first? What is the business plan of the program? A flow chart of the administration, simulated coverage, and medical services needs to be drafted. After healthcare reform passes, how long before it is implemented?

Has a Frequently Asked Questions (FAQ) been developed? There are many common questions the newly insured will have? Those without insurance usually go to community clinics, emergency rooms, and local doctors. How will the monitoring of these locations take place? What tracking is being considered for the expected reduction in cost, time, and staffing?

Is a standard of care being developed for the selected physicians, labs, and insurance firms? In addition, what is the selection process for private and HMO firms? They will want to get a set percentage of income or patients (this is based on my experience in the healthcare industry). Now we have the opportunity to improve service and patient care expectations. HMO's have a reputation for assembly line treatment. Will this issue be addressed in the new standards of care expected? Do we collect the monies from the funding sources based on each group that will be serviced? Will it be done on a quarterly base? Afterwards will the groups to be serviced be selected?

The proposal by Sen. Kent Conrad, D-N.D, *Dems advance proposal to spread health coverage* by David Espo, AP Special Correspondent 6/9/09, regarding a nonprofit cooperative would need to be factored into the current frame work. Consider it a possible alternative to the government run and funded universal healthcare for the non-insured. What types of tax credits or deferred income and expenditures will they be given?

Currently the 1040 Form Schedule A allows for some medical deductions based on Adjusted Gross Income (AGI). Will the amount allowed be reduced or increased? Factor in the health cost and/or health related physicals, lab work, and initial medical cost. Most of those uninsured will require extensive physicals, lab work, and treatment for illness (existing and developing). How will a priority of cost and required medical treatments be determined? This initial cost is one that may cost more than expected given the recent statistics on obesity.

These are just some of the FAQs others and I have. The president and those opposing the healthcare reform have not addressed these areas. The sooner these and other questions which will arise are addressed, the greater the possibility for more support and speedy implementation.

It would be a good idea to request the advice and experience of countries that currently do operate a government run healthcare program. We need their model to start and improve upon. It will also improve our public relations with them. This is in addition to getting the global support we desperately need.

The next healthcare reform town halls update needs to be on a Saturday or Sunday afternoon or evening. Having it during the week, like the last one was, is not good planning or implementation. You need the viewership of those who have to work given the economic downsizing that continues. During the week, they have a set sleep schedule. It usually starts from 8pm to 11pm.

You need their undivided attention to comfort their concerns and doubts. This new change has long been needed.

July 27, 2009

Improving the Next Press Conference on Healthcare Support

Please include the following information in your preparation and presentation. It will help you gain support by the public, the house of representative, the senate, and others:

Include charts and graphs showing before and after scenarios:

1. Of the financial challenges that will be created/and resolved with the passage of health care reform.
2. Of the quality of life improvements, challenges, and the reduced health care costs.
3. Have representatives of the various segments share their pro/con with supportive data and suggestions that you and the public can hear first – hand.
4. Show a sample demographic of the actual citizens who will benefit or need the healthcare reform passed. Have them tell their story to the nation like you did when you were running for office.
5. Of those who oppose your specifics have them present alternatives, have them show the areas. Specify what compromises both parties are willing to make to get something passed.

Because the health care reform proposal is over 1,000 pages, it may be wise to focus on the most important top 10, 20, or 50 areas for passage. You will win greater support with the country and your colleagues in D.C. Trying to include everything in one reform may cause less not more support. The country knows that there will be a need for additional changes. They are willing to wait or deal with those areas after the initial health care reform is underway.

As I stated in my last letter, I found out last week and this weekend, experts and media analysts support my suggestions. They agree to help you present yourself and the cause at its very best. Please review Katie Couric and, Bob Schieffer's comments from *CBS News* and George Stephanopoulos from *ABC news*. They both suggest as I did. You need to include the details of the healthcare plan. As they say the "devil is in the details."

You need to act as if the plan has been approved and share what will happen next. Apply the format you used in the election campaign. You shared information of the presidential operations under your management. That example would apply to any cause you want/need passed at this point. One good point I noticed. You mentioned two common people's need for this cause to get speedy approval.

Also it is very important that you discontinue scaring the viewers of how much more they will pay. That is a given, no need to repeat it. Instead show with realistic statistics how it will decrease. What things can our citizens do to help reduce it? For example, exercising more and applying healthier eating habits. Incorporating the selection of good foods that contribute to their good health. In addition include what specific features of your personal health care benefits you want to include for the country's uninsured.

Be sure to include accomplishments. Have your direct report give updates on old issues that are helping the economy. We need as much as possible positive feedback. It will keep the momentum towards recovery going.

January 19, 2010

Improving Airport Security

Security jobs at our airports are to be considered temporary or transitional career moves. This is a job choice made by those seeking transitional employment. It provides easy entrance to temporary employment for just enough time to pay the absolute minimal living expenses. Sometimes it is used to fill the time while one's true calling is discovered. If not, than a job that offers better pay and/or benefits.

The human resource department needs to plan on a high turnover rate for these positions. There will be a need for continuous replacements and on call staffing. This is not something the applicant will admit. Their intent is to get employed long enough to find a job to their true calling or with better compensation. They cannot afford to be honest. Employers do not want to be the transient job while one searches for a better job.

Here are my recommendations to improve airport security and avoid a repeat of the December 2009 events:

1. Only allow security guards to have company provided cell phones for work related emergencies. If they are allowed to have access to their personal cell phones, they will use it and become involved in the call. This applies whether they are bored or it is a true personal emergency call.

This puts those who rely on them for protection to be put in harm's way. Instead provide a central call location where they can check their messages during breaks. The time spread would be one every two hours and at least a one hour lunch. This location needs to offer them the privacy and accommodations (a writing place with pad and pen/pencil) where they can check in periodically for personal calls.

2. Put additional cameras at the entrance and exist throughout the airports. To cover the cost, have it allocated between passengers, airlines, and foreign countries that use our airports. Include security related costs for those who have or are known to promote terrorists commuting to and from our country.

3. Have a rotating security group view the cameras in one to two hours intervals to maintain concentration. This applies both to those watching passengers and those going through baggage. No more than 3 to 4 hours should be spent at a station. This will help security guards maintain a higher level of focus then is currently available.

The security guards cannot be allowed to leave their post without a supervisor's approval. There will have to be a stand in guard at their post until they return and before they leave their post. This includes all reasons for moving away from their post such as bathroom breaks, smoking, and/or meal breaks.

4. Have a camera on the security guards and use an outside security consulting company to review the tapes daily. There should also be a back-up for tape repairs and/or replacements at all times.

5. Make multi-language announcements advising passengers to report other passengers who create security problems or behave unusual.

6. Provide a greeting and departure area for those who need more time to spend with their loved ones. It would be available before going through security screening and/or boarding. Arrivals and departures are very hard for some. We saw the emotional toll it took on the foreign passenger.

He was willing to violate security just to spend time with his loved one. They are overtaken by their emotions when dealing with the temporary departure (lost) of a loved one.

7. Those on the terrorist watch list should get extra screening and as President Obama stated. An undercover marshal should be on board in the flights they use. To reduce the cost, a group travel airplane should be required for those who travel on the same date. Another option is assessing an additional fee to their flight purchase. This fee would only be assessed if their country's government is not willing to help with the security cost the U.S. and airports will incur.

8. Additional quick screening of those on the watch list. It would involve required finger printing and scanning at the airport. These should be cross referenced with established terror threats to the U.S. and other countries. It would be selectively shared information with our alliances.

9. Have random audits of security cameras through an outside consulting security company. This will avoid the embarrassing situation the TSA management caused during the Christmas holiday event.

10. There is a history of airport terrorist choosing holidays and high traffic areas. Increase the security guard manpower during holidays and at high traffic areas throughout the year.

11. As one congressional or senate representative stated on the news "terrorist should not have an attorney provided when there is proof of their attempt to destroy our country and/or people." Taxpayers do not want their monies going to defend someone who wants to kills them! Please do not offer this legal service.

12. Recently (within the past week), a special investigative news report was done on airport security by WPIX Channel 11 News in New York. The report showed their staff was able to gain access to restricted/authorized areas. This was at a

terminal in one of New York City's airports. They informed the TSA personnel of the discovered access. The entrances for authorized personnel have been overlooked by TSA. This is an area that needs just as much security as the baggage and passenger screening areas.

References

Introduction & July 27, 2009

1. *CBS Evening News.* Host Katie Couric & Bob Schieffer. CBS. WCBS, New York, New York. July 2009. *"The devil is in the details."*

September 2008 World Financial Crisis – The Lost Letter
2. Rick Warren, *"Decade of Destiny,"* Saddleback Church, Lake Forest, CA.
   Last modified Winter 2012. Accessed 2012.
   www.saddlebackchurch.com

10-06-08 Bailout Suggestions
3. Aaron Task. "Yahoo Finance," *Finally, Relief for Homeowners: BofA Settles Predatory Lending Suit,* Oct. 06, 2008. Retrieved July 2012.
   http://finance.yahoo.com/tech-ticker/article/88871/Finally-Relief-for-Homeowners-BofA-Settles-Predatory-Lending-Suit

10-06-08 Bailout Suggestions
4. Julie H. Davis, "Yahoo News," *Congress hears Lehman sought millions for execs*, Associated Press, Oct. 06, 2008. Retrieved July 2012.
   http://news.yahoo.com/s/ap/20081006/ap_on_go_co/meltdown_lehman

11-05-08 Tentative Agenda for November 2008 World Economic Summit

5. Christopher Bodeen, "USA Today," *Asia, Europe reach consensus on financial crisis,* Associated Press, October 25, 2008. Retrieved July 2012.
   http://www.usatoday.com/money/economy/2008-10-24-1195703154_x.htm

11-05-08 Tentative Agenda for November 2008 World Economic Summit

6. *"Inside Edition,"* "More Outrage for Bigwigs at AIG," air date 03-07-2009 (New York: Channel 5/WFOX, 2009), Television. Retrieved July 2012.
   http://www.insideedition.com/news/2733/more-outrage-for-bigwigs-at-aig.aspx

11-05-08 Tentative Agenda for November 2008 World Economic Summit

7. Randolph A. Pohlman, *"VDM - Value-Driven Management,"* Last modified 97-01 June, 1997. Accessed Fall 2008.
   http://www.huizenga.nova.edu/5095/vdm.cfm

12-09-08 $25 Billion Auto Loan With Conditions

8. Fitch, *"Auto sales to fall 10.7 percent in 2009,"* Associated Press, Dec. 09, 2008.

01-04-09 Stimulus Package sent to Speaker Pelosi

9. Senate Majority Leader Harry Reid, D-Nev. *Stimulus Package.* Video release 2008 or 2009. Fox News Sunday. Television.

01-18-09 Reversal of Bailout Through The Presidential Power

10. *"Obama-Biden Transition Project."* (Accessed 2008 or 2009; site now discontinued).
    http://change.gov

03-18-09 AIG Bonuses Issues

11. George Stephanopoulos, *This Week with George Stephanopoulos,* performed by George Stephanopoulos (New York: Channel 7.1/WABC, 2009), Television

03-18-09 AIG Bonuses Issues

12. *"Inside Edition,"* "More Outrage for Bigwigs at AIG," air date 03-07-2009 (New York: Channel 5/WFOX, 2009), Television. Retrieved July 2012.
http://www.insideedition.com/news/2733/more-outrage-for-bigwigs-at-aig.aspx

06-24-09 Citi's Self Imposed Pay Raise

13. Stephen Bernard & Ieva M. Augstums (contributor). "NBC News Business," *Citi boosting salaries to offset lower bonuses,* Associated Press, Jun 24, 2009. Retrieved July 2012.
http://www.nbcnewyork.com/news/business/Citi-Boosting-Salaries-to-Offset-Lower-Bonuses-.html

06-24-09 Citi's Self Imposed Pay Raise

14. Marshall Sylver, *Passion, Profit, and Power* (New York: Simon & Schuster, 1995), p 100.

07-13-09 Logistics for Health Care Reform

15. David Espo, *"Dems advance proposal to spread health coverage,"* Associated Press, Jun 09, 2009.

07-27-09 & Introduction – Improving the Next Press Conference on Healthcare Support

16. *CBS Evening News.* Host Katie Couric & Bob Schieffer. CBS. WCBS, New York, New York. July 2009. *"The devil is in the details."*

07-27-09 & Introduction – Improving the Next Press Conference on Healthcare Support

17. *ABC Evening News*. Host George Stephanopoulos. ABC. WABC, New York, New York.
July 2009. *"The devil is in the details."*

01-19-10 Improving Airport Security

18. Meredith Traina, *Schumer Urges Airlines To Avoid Lax Airports*. (New York: Channel 11/WPIX, 2010), Television

Conclusion

19. Napoleon Hill, *Think and Grow Rich*. (Connecticut: Ralston Publishing Co., 1937).

Conclusion

20. Dale Carnegie, *How to Win Friends and Influence People* (New York: Simon and Schuster, Inc. 1937).

Conclusion

21. Kerry Patterson & Joseph Grenny, *Influencer: The Power to Change Anything* (Ohio: McGraw – Hill, 2007).

Conclusion

22. K Patterson, J Grenny, R McMillian, and A Switzler, *Crucial Conversations* (Ohio: McGraw – Hill, 2002).

Conclusion

To review, we need to play an active role in creating changes. Each and every one of us was created to make a difference. The purpose for our time on earth is to leave a legacy. It can be small or large. We can use our talents, emotions, experience, or education. Any of these will propelle us to do things we thought we could not but find we can.

It takes a test or a need to see change. I did not believe at first that these events happened to test my dedication to our country. My desire to prevent our country from financial disaster caused me to make use of my education and experiences.

God and I want you to use your true-life examples and inspiration to make a difference.

Our country can only be improved with your participation.

You may also wish to read the following books that helped me become an advisor and advocate:

1. Think and Grow Rich by Napoleon Hills
2. How to Win Friends and Influence People by Dale Carnegie
3. Influencer: The Power to Change Anything by Kerry Patterson & Joseph Grenny
4. Crucial Conversations by K Patterson, J Grenny, R McMillian, and A Switzler

We can only be better or do better when we challenge the purpose things and events in our lives have.

Please do your part to service our country. You do not have to join the military, just share you insight, inspiration, and information for a better America. Our leaders await your comments, compliments, and/or complaints.

Why I Wrote This Book

There were three compelling factors:

1. Fixing what seemed at the time as a simple meeting so I could return to work.
2. Being a workaholic and seeing what it is like to go on an unwanted vacation. It was more painful than I had expected.
3. Taking what seemed at the time to be the hardest school subject, this event would provide a true life extra credit assignment. I would also be able to show actual use of school work. It would ensure a passing grade.

Being a part of history by influencing change that made a difference was something I had learned from the movies.

It would also look great on the resume.

After all, it is a tough sell explaining a six-month vacation, at the start of the Great Recession.

MARIA E ACOSTA

OBJECTIVE: Advisor to Government Officials, Constituents, and Industry Leaders during The Great Recession & Recovery

- Coached industry and constituents on government and business strategies
- Collaborated, persuaded, and tutored politicians, the business community, and voters
- Created what if scenarios as a form of persuasion to gain support and participation
- Educated, enlightened, influenced, informed, and inspired for a united front
- Guided and educated in layperson language on: taxes, government, economics, and business operations
- Offered crises management skills and methods
- Provided techniques and steps for cooperation, encouragement, and training
- Shared and explained use of the tax system as part of the stimulus package(s)
- Used innovative thinking in crises, strategic planning, and execution

ACCOUNTING, EXECUTIVE & TAX ASSISTANT SKILLS
2008 to Present

Situation, Task, Action, and Results (*STAR format)

1. Auto Bailout

S –   The auto industry has suffered many years of poor management.

   During The Great Recession most business lenders were reluctant to offer loans.

   They lacked: capital, credit, and creativity in sales, marketing, and advertising.

T –   Persuaded our government and constituents to use taxpayer monies as business loans.

A –   Educated and informed our government, constituents, and the auto industry staff.

   Shared, knowledge, techniques, and values on company operations and presentations.

R –   The auto industry was able to re-establish a prominent precedence in sales, marketing, and advertising.

   Provided businesses and management insight and information.

   Guided government and industry leaders through improved quality and customer oriented techniques.

   Persuaded our government leaders to offer consumers car purchase tax credits.

2. Global Financial Crisis

S – The U.S. and foreign countries were blaming each other for The Great Recession.

Each felt the other bared responsibility and action for possible financial ruins.

T – Used transferable industry skills.

Demonstrated knowledge in: economics, taxes, and as an executive and accounting assistant.

Provided mediation, transitional, and temporary solution(s).

A – Provided a tentative emergency meeting agenda for world leaders.

Included a win/win meeting format on crises management.

Role played devil's advocate and acted as a neutral and consumer liaison.

Shared project management and interpersonal skills to gain participation and alliances.

R – Improved our country foreign relations.

Demonstrated use of industry and transferable proactive and problem solving skills.

Contributed management advice that diminished effects of the global and U.S. financial crises.

3. Stimulus Packages

S – Our country's business operations are falling behind
foreign competitors.

They have discarded strategic planning, training, and
education.

T – Shared insight, information, and logistics on rebuilding
U.S. companies.

Educated our leaders and the business community on
standards, practices, consumer services, credit alternatives,
and employee relations.

A – Provided a grocery list of areas lacking.

Shared management and strategic planning skills.

Contributed experience and knowledge in economics,
accounting, executive management, and taxes.

Incorporated my knowledge in training and teaching
citizens and leaders.

Used transferrable skills as a tax preparer, and as a bilingual
(English/Spanish) executive and accounting assistant.

Presented in layperson language, use of the tax system to
stimulate spending during The Great Recession.

R – Gained support from the former and current U.S.
presidents, the senate, and the congress on stimulus
package(s) spending.

Secured tax credit for training and hiring the displaced and
unemployed work force.

*The STAR work style description provides a general analysis and
informative format of problem solving and management skills. It
specifies a **Situation**, the **Task** to handle it, the **Action** implemented,
and the **Results** gained.*

*It gives insight into the approach taken, skills applied, and
accomplished achieved or challenges conquered.*

PROFESSIONAL EXPERIENCE
Book Writer – 2008 to Present

- Working on final edits for book on consumer and economic challenges during The Great Recession and Recovery. Secured publishing company. Estimated release date 2nd to 3rd quarter of 2013.

2004 to Present
EDUCATION

2010 to Present
North Orange County Community College – School of Continuing Education, Anaheim, CA
Microsoft Office (Word, Excel, PowerPoint, Access, Publisher) and, QuickBooks

2009
New Jersey City University, Jersey City, NJ
B.S. – Business Administration – Accounting

Supplemental Information - available upon request
- Book Sample Introduction Topics –
  The Great Recession & Recover

Bibliography

Bernard, Stephen & Augstums Ieva M. (contributor). "NBC News Business," *Citi boosting salaries to offset lower bonuses,* Associated Press, Jun 24, 2009. Retrieved July 2012.
http://www.nbcnewyork.com/news/business/Citi-Boosting-Salaries-to-Offset-Lower-Bonuses-.html

Bodeen, Christopher. "USA Today," *Asia, Europe reach consensus on financial crisis,* Associated Press, October 25, 2008. Retrieved July 2012.
http://www.usatoday.com/money/economy/2008-10-24-1195703154_x.htm

CBS Evening News. Host Katie Couric & Bob Schieffer. CBS. WCBS, New York, New York. July 2009. "*The devil is in the details.*" Television.

Carnegie, Dale. *How to Win Friends and Influence People.* New York: Simon and Schuster, Inc. 1937.

Davis, Julie H. "Yahoo News," *Congress hears Lehman sought millions for execs,* Associated Press, Oct 06, 2008. Retrieved July 2012.
http://news.yahoo.com/s/ap/20081006/ap_on_go_co/meltdown_lehman

Espo, David. "*Dems advance proposal to spread health coverage,*" Associated Press, 09 Jun 2009

Fitch. "*Auto sales to fall 10.7 percent in 2009.*" Associated Press, Dec. 09, 2008.

Hill, Napoleon. *Think and Grow Rich*. Connecticut: Ralston Publishing Co., 1937.

Inside Edition. *"More Outrage for Bigwigs at AIG."* Air date 03-07-2009. (New York: Channel 5/WFOX, 2009), Television. Retrieved July 2012.
    http://www.insideedition.com/news/2733/more-outrage-for-bigwigs-at-aig.aspx

Obama-Biden Transition Project." (Accessed 2008 or 2009; site now discontinued).
    http://change.gov

Patterson, K & Grenny, J, McMillian, R, and Switzler, A. *Crucial Conversations*. Ohio: McGraw – Hill, 2002.

Patterson, Kerry & Grenny Joseph. *Influencer: The Power to Change Anything*. Ohio: McGraw – Hill, 2007.

Pohlman, Randolph A. *"VDM - Value-Driven Management."* Last modified 97-01 June, 1997. Accessed fall 2008.
    http://www.huizenga.nova.edu/5095/vdm.cfm

Reid, Harry – Senate Majority Leader. D – Nev. *Stimulus Package*. Video release 2008 or 2009. Fox News Sunday. Television

Stephanopoulo, George. *This Week with George Stephanopoulos*. Performed by George Stephanopoulos. 2009, New York: Channel 7.1/WABC. Television.

Sylver, Marshall. *Passion, Profit, and Power*. New York: Simon & Schuster, 1995.

Task, Aaron. "Yahoo Finance," *Finally, Relief for Homeowners: BofA Settles PredatoryLending Suit,"* Oct. 06, 2008. Retrieved July 2012. http://finance.yahoo.com/tech-ticker/article/88871/Finally-Relief-for-Homeowners-BofA-Settles-Predatory-Lending-Suit

Traina, Meredith, *Schumer Urges Airlines to Avoid Lax Airports,* (New York: Channel 11/WPIX, 2010), Television.

Warren, Rick. *"Decade of Destiny,"* Saddleback Church, Lake Forest, CA. Last modified Winter 2012. Accessed 2012. www.saddlebackchurch.com

About the Author

Born in La Havana Cuba the author came to the U.S. with her mother. The flight to the U.S. was one of the last direct flights allowed by the Cuban reign. Like many Cubans before and after her, she quickly adapted to the environment. Learning the language and losing the accent was the most difficult of all her challenges to overcome.

As many true life and fictional characters in made for TV movies, like Eva Peron, Norma Rae and, Erin Brokavich, she had the opportunity to make a difference.

Few events in recent history mirror The Great Depression. Of course, there was that six month of unwanted vacation that convinced her, she had to do something about what would be known as The Great Recession.

Was it timing or destiny to stand front and center by the TV when the global financial crisis was announced? This was God's way of giving her something to test and use. She Often wondered what and when she would use her life and work lessons. What was the purpose of all that unused knowledge? These events would finally give her a role of a life time. This major event provided the opportunity to put her education, life, and work experience to good use. Our country needed her and of course it would fill that resume major gap.

It was the least she could do to serve her country. Also it would put her to work for a worthy cause. This opportunity helped her apply her knowledge in true life changing events. It was considered a simple problem to her at first. Providing guidance for an emergency world leaders meeting was second nature, given the many years of handling corporate executive and direct reports. At the time, it seemed something that could be resolved quickly.

This event was novel, interesting and made her available to share her influence, knowledge, and experience.

She has 20 plus years of work experience as a bilingual (English/ Spanish) executive and accounting assistant. The years of exposure dealing with crisis and problem solving at almost every temporary assignment she had were put to good use for our country.

Pass Accomplishment

During the early 1990s, Maria E Acosta was a catalyst for credit reform. The credit challenges of false, incorrect, and misleading information on her credit reports gave way to many changes. For starters, credit agencies had to accept the fact that putting incorrect information would not be tolerated. People were given the opportunity to correct or provide their side of the story. There were errors the agencies would not admit or correct themselves on personal credit reports.

This began the requirement for consumers to get a free annual credit report. With the help of a consumer credit, not-for-profit, agency in Henderson Pennsylvania, she was able to get the media exposure. This helped her get the agencies to fix some of the problems on her credit reports.

She was featured on the front page of the Orange County Register in 1991. That was followed by an interviewed on KABC Channel 7 TV, (Los Angeles, California) with TV anchor, Paul Dandridge on a credit issues segment.

During her college years, she was involved in student government. She provided many suggestions that were implemented on academic changes, improving the school's safety and, environment.

Professional Experience

In the early 1980s, she worked with the IRS Volunteer Income Tax Assistance (VITA) program. This was where most of her tax knowledge was acquired. She later worked for Jackson Hewitt Income Tax Service for about 4 years doing taxes for low income and small businesses.

After working as a teacher assistant for the Los Angeles Unified she pursued work as a temporary employee doing accounting, administrative, data entry, human resources, payroll, and customer service for small, medium, and large companies. This is where most of her problem solving and executive level experience where attained.

Education

She struggled for many years to get a permanent job due to her lack of a college degree. Once she was able to gain sponsorship, she acquired her B.S. in Business Administration with a major in Accounting from New Jersey City University in Jersey City, New Jersey.

She currently attends the School of Continuing Education to improve and maintain her software skills.